Edith Stein

Selected Writings by Edith Stein
(Sr. Teresia Benedicta a Cruce OCD).

With Comments and Reminiscences

by Susanne M. Batzdorff.

EDITH STEIN
Selected Writings

*With Comments, Reminiscences
and Translations of her
Prayers and Poems
by her niece*

Susanne M. Batzdorff

TEMPLEGATE PUBLISHERS

First published in the United States of America by:
Templegate Publishers
302 East Adams Street
P.O. Box 5152
Springfield, IL 62705

Manufactured in the United States of America

ISBN 0-87243-189-4

Contents

List of Photographs

Edith Stein, 1926

Preface

Among the autobiographical sketches of Edith Stein her account "How I Came to the Cologne Carmel," is surely one of the most interesting. It forms the center of this volume around which the rest of the material is grouped.

Edith Stein wrote this account about two weeks before her transfer from Cologne to the village of Echt, Netherlands, and gave these pages to her prioress, Sr. Teresia Renata de Spiritu Sancto (Posselt) for Christmas 1938. These remarks are subtitled "A contribution to the history of the Carmel in Cologne." Doubtless her remarks constitute such a contribution; but above all, they are a contribution to the story of her own life.

One expects an historical account to contain dates, names, and facts. And indeed, Edith Stein includes an abundance of these. These data alone assure the reader of something compelling, especially that reader to whom the time and place of these events are familiar. But something more profound must resonate in them, to make this essay so uniquely moving.

These reminiscences are the reflections of a human being standing at a crossroads. Sören Kierkegaard once said that life is lived forward but understood backward. We do not know whether Edith Stein—who as a young woman occupied herself with the study of Kierkegaard—knew this quotation. It is, however, *her* situation which he expresses. We do not know the life that lies ahead of us; first we must live it. But we can surely try, indeed we must try to understand what has already become *our* life. And that can only happen in retrospect. When that hindsight is more than a fleeting backward glance, when it is an attentive search for comprehension of "how it all came about," then that will enable us to take our place in the Now. And from that position in the present, our life will receive its forward direction; we gain a new perspective. A new understanding for what was and what became of it, can be awakened, a new understanding for what is to come, because the present

9

grows out of the past and forms a unified whole together with that which is still to be.

The Archives of our Cologne Carmel include the handwritten manuscript of Edith Stein's brief treatise "How I Came to the Cologne Carmel." It consists of forty-two pages, hand-numbered by the author herself. Above the title the Roman numeral - I - can clearly be seen. Apparently Edith Stein intended to write a sequel to this first "Contribution to the history of the Cologne Carmel." As far as we have been able to determine so far, she never had a chance to accomplish this. But the text we have in hand has much to tell us. Upon her departure from Cologne, Edith Stein made an attempt to tie the yet unknown and very precarious future to the already familiar, already accomplished, successfully passed events and to shape it all in advance into a meaningful whole. It is the moving testimony of a human being who has rendered to herself an account of her life's course, and who knows within her heart that this course will continue.

When Edith Stein entered Carmel, she surely stood at one of the crossroads of her life. In the first few lines of her essay, she herself says that she sees a connection between the new beginning then (in October, 1933) and the present event (five years later). What Edith Stein then saw ahead as a piece of the future shrouded in darkness, we can now recognize in retrospect. The essay by Susanne Batzdorff née Biberstein, the niece Edith Stein mentioned in her writings and loved very much, helps us to attain an overview of this unusual life in its entirety. The poems by Edith Stein, written during the last part of her life and found among her unpublished papers, tell us how this Carmelite, as a devout Christian, sought to cope with her fate. The last chapter in this book, written by a devout Jew, shows us the monumental task (which we Christians failed to pursue for centuries): To build unity through reconciliation and understanding with those who, together with us, believe in our Father in Heaven.

Sr. Maria Amata Neyer OCD.
Cologne.

Translator's Note

For the translation of all Biblical passages the text of the Jerusalem Bible has been used.

Several of the poems in the original German edition were rendered in abridged form. We were fortunate to obtain the complete authenticated texts through the courtesy of Sister Maria Amata Neyer OCD, Curator of the *Edith-Stein-Archiv*, Carmelite Monastery "Maria vom Frieden," Cologne, Germany in the form of photostatic copies of the handwritten texts by Edith Stein. Where these were no longer available, typescript copies from the *Archiv* were used. They are published here in their entirety for the first time. The German text of the following poems is that of the edition published by Kaffke:

Aus meinem Herzen strömt die Weise	A festive song streams from my heart
Erhör, o Gott, mein Flehen	God, hear me, I implore you
In aller Stürme Toben	Whenever storms are roaring
Jauchzet, ihr Völker	Rejoice, ye nations.

The remaining poems are given in their complete versions as found in manuscript form in the Archives in Cologne and are translated from these texts. The photographs in the book are from our family's collection.

To Sister Maria Amata Neyer I offer my sincere gratitude for her valuable suggestions to ensure the accuracy of these texts and background information as well as for her willingness to put these copies of the original texts at my disposal. I must also thank Sister Josephine Koeppel of Carmel Thornbrow, Elysburg, Pennsylvania, for reading the manuscript of *How I Came to the Cologne Carmel*. She reviewed the text and offered valuable advice with regard to authentic nomenclature and idiom.

Edith Stein, the author of these poems and prayers, said that a translator must be like a pane of clear glass, letting the writer's own words be seen as plainly as possible. I have tried to do this, but there were passages which could not be rendered exactly while simultaneously preserving poetic form and rhythm.

Edith Stein was my cherished aunt, sister of my mother, and as I work with her writings, I find myself wishing that I could discuss them with her. That privilege I cannot have. The next best thing is to concentrate on the words of the text and to let my memory return to those times, many decades back, when I was able to speak to her and she could answer my questions. The contact I establish in this way appears at times to be close and intimate. I beg her forgiveness as well as the reader's if I have in some instances failed to be the "clear pane of glass" through which the light of her words may shine.

Susanne M. Batzdorff

How I Came to the Cologne Carmel

*A Contribution to the History of the Carmel in Cologne
translated from the German by
Susanne M. Batzdorff*

Edith Stein, 1931

I.

How I Came to the Cologne Carmel

Perhaps I shall leave this house soon after Christmas. The circumstances which have forced us to initiate my transfer to Echt (Holland) are strikingly reminiscent of the situation at the time of my entrance into the Carmel. It is likely that there is a subtle connection between the two.

When the Third Reich was established early in the year 1933, I had been an instructor at the German Institute for Scientific Pedagogy in Münster, Westphalia for about a year. I lived in the "Collegium Marianum" amidst a large number of nuns who were students and who belonged to the most diverse orders as well as a small group of other women students, lovingly taken care of by the Sisters of our Lady.

One evening during the vacation I returned late from a meeting of the Society of Catholic Academics. I don't know whether I had forgotten to take my house key or whether there was a key stuck in the lock from the inside. At any rate, I could not get in. I tried to lure someone to the window by ringing the bell and clapping hands, but in vain. The women students who lived in the rooms facing the street were already away on vacation. A passerby asked whether he could help me. When I turned to him, he bowed deeply and said, "Dr. Stein, I didn't recognize you." He was a Catholic teacher who was a participant in a workshop sponsored by the Institute. He excused himself for a moment to tell his wife, who had gone ahead with another lady. He exchanged a few words with her and then returned to me.

"My wife would like to invite you to spend the night at our house."

That was a good solution, and I accepted gratefully. They took me to a simple house in the style of Münster's middle class. We sat down in the living room. The amiable lady of the house put a bowl of fruit on the table and left in order to prepare a room for me. The man began a conversation in which he related what American newspapers had reported concerning cruelties to which Jews had been subjected. They were unconfirmed reports; and so I do not wish to repeat them. I am only interested in the impression I got that evening. True, I had heard of rigorous measures against the Jews before. But now a light dawned in my brain that once again God had put a heavy hand upon His people and that the fate of this people would also be mine. I did not allow the man who sat opposite me to notice what was going on inside of me. Apparently he did not know about my Jewish descent. In similar cases, I would usually enlighten the others immediately. This time I did not do it. It would have seemed to me like a breach of their hospitality if I had disturbed their night's rest by such a revelation.

On Thursday of Passion Week, I traveled to Beuron. Since 1928 I had spent that week and the Easter holiday there each year and had quietly held my own private retreat. This time a special reason drew me there. During the past weeks I had constantly given thought to whether I could do something about the plight of the Jews. Finally I had made a plan to travel to Rome and to ask the Holy Father in a private audience for an encyclical. But I did not want to take such a step on my own. Years ago I had taken private vows. Since I had found a kind of monastic home in Beuron, I was permitted to regard Archabbot Raphael[1] as "my abbot" and to put before him all important problems for his judgment. It was not certain, however, that I would find him there. In early January he had gone on a trip to Japan. But I knew that he would do his utmost to be at home during Passion week.

Although it suited my nature to make such an overt move, I sensed that this was not yet "of the essence." But I did not yet know what this "essence" really was. I interrupted my travels in Cologne from Thursday afternoon until Friday morning. I was instructing a catechumen there, and had to devote some time to her at every possible opportunity. I wrote and asked her to find out where we could attend the Holy Hour in the evening. It was the eve of the First

1   Dr. Raphael Josef Walzer, 1888—1966, Archabbot of the Benedictine monastery of Beuron. Abbot Walzer had to flee from the Nazis and spent many years abroad, in the United States, North Africa and elsewhere. He returned to Germany after World War II and resided in the Abbey of Neuburg near Heidelberg. He died in Heidelberg.

16

Friday of April, and in this Holy Year, 1933[2], the memory of the passion of our Lord was being observed with particular solemnity everywhere. At 8 o'clock in the evening, we arrived for the Holy Hour at the Carmel Cologne—Lindental. A priest (it was Father Wüsten[3], Vicar at the Cathedral, as I learned later) gave a homily and announced that from then on this worship service would be held there every Thursday. He spoke beautifully and movingly, but something other than his words occupied me more intensely. I talked with the Savior and told Him that I knew that it was His cross that was now being placed upon the Jewish people; that most of them did not understand this, but that those who did, would have to take it up willingly in the name of all. I would do that. He should only show me how. At the end of the service, I was certain that I had been heard. But what this carrying of the cross was to consist in, that I did not yet know.

Next morning I continued my trip to Beuron. When I changed trains that evening in Immendingen[4], I met P. Aloys Mager[5]. We spent the last part of the trip together. Soon after we said hello, he reported as Beuron's most important news item: Father Archabbot had returned from Japan that very morning in good health. So that, too, was in order.

Through my inquiries in Rome I ascertained that because of the tremendous crowds I would have no chance for a private audience. At best I might be admitted to a "semi-private audience," i.e. an audience in a small group. That did not serve my purpose. I abandoned my travel plans and instead presented my request in writing. I know that my letter was delivered to the Holy Father[6] unopened; some time thereafter I received his blessing for myself and for my relatives. Nothing else happened. Later on I often wondered whether this letter might have come to his mind once in a while. For in the years that followed, that which I had predicted for the future of the Catholics in Germany came true step by step.

2 1933 was considered the 1900th anniversary year of the death of Jesus Christ. Thus this year was singled out for pilgrimages to Rome and other holy places, e.g. the Cathedral of Trier. See also Footnote 12.
3 Hubert Wüsten, 1891—1962, Curate at the Cologne Cathedral from 1926 to 1935.
4 Railroad station near Beuron. Even today a point where passengers change trains.
5 Pater Aloys Mager OSB, 1883—1946, known as an outstanding teacher and author, he was a member of the Benedictine Order. A professor of philosophy and experimental psychology, he acquired some renown through his research on the psychology of mysticism, with special emphasis on Teresa of Avila.
6 Pope Pius XI (Ambrogio Damiano Achille Ratti; pontificate 1922—Feb. 10, 1939).

Prior to my departure I asked Father Archabbot what I should do if I had to give up my work in Münster. He found it totally unbelievable that that could happen. On my return trip to Münster I read a newspaper article about a big National Socialist teachers' meeting in which the religious teachers' organizations were also forced to participate. It became clear to me that in the field of education one would least tolerate influences which were contrary to the ruling policy. The Institute in which I worked was purely Catholic, co-founded and supported by the Catholic Teachers' Organization. Thus its days were probably numbered. All the more I would have to reckon with the termination of my short career as a college instructor. On April 19 I returned to Münster; next day I went to the Institute. The director was on a vacation trip in Greece. The administrator, a Catholic teacher, took me into the office and told me his troubles. For weeks he had been involved in upsetting negotiations; he was totally worn out.

"Imagine, Doctor Stein, somebody even came and said, 'Dr. Stein isn't going to continue teaching, is she?' "

He considered it best if I would refrain from scheduling any lectures for this summer and just do some quiet research in the Marianum[7]. By autumn the situation would settle down, perhaps the Church would take over the Institute. In that case nothing would prevent me from resuming my activities. I accepted this information very calmly. I attached no importance to the hopes he held out.

"If I can't go on here," I said, "then there's no possibility for me in Germany any more."

The administrator expressed his admiration for me for seeing things so clearly, even though I lived as a recluse and paid no attention to worldly matters.

I felt almost relieved that I was now caught up in the common fate. I had to decide, however, what I should now do with myself. I consulted the opinion of the chairwoman of the Catholic Teachers' Organization. It was at her suggestion that I had gone to Münster. She advised me to spend at least the summer in Münster and to continue working on a research paper I had started. The Organization would pay my subsistence, because the results of my research would be useful to them. If it should be impossible to resume my work at the Institute, I could, later on, look into opportunities abroad. Very soon thereafter I did in fact receive an offer from South America. But by that time, a very different path had been revealed to me.

7 Collegium Marianum, a dormitory for students inhabited predominantly by women religious. Edith Stein lived there while on the faculty of the Institute.

About ten days after my return from Beuron, the idea occurred to me: Might not now the time be ripe to enter Carmel? For almost twelve years, Carmel had been my goal; since summer 1921, when the *Life* of our Holy Mother Teresa had happened to fall into my hands and had put an end to my long search for the true faith. When on New Year's Day 1922 I received the Sacrament of Baptism, I thought that this was merely the preparation for entering the Order. But a few months later, when for the first time since my baptism I stood face to face with my dear mother, it became clear to me that she would not be able to withstand this second blow for the time being. She would not die of it, but it would fill her with such bitterness that I could not take the responsibility for that. I would have to wait patiently. My spiritual counselors assured me of this over and over. Lately this waiting had become very hard for me. I had become a stranger in the outside world. Before I began my job in Münster and after the first semester I had urgently pleaded for permission to enter the order. It was denied me with reference to my mother and because of the effectiveness which my work had had in Catholic circles in recent years. I had yielded. But now the walls that had stood in my way had crumbled. My effectiveness was at an end. And surely my mother would prefer me to be in a convent in Germany rather than a school in South America. On April 30, — it was the Sunday of the Good Shepherd — the Feast of St. Ludger was observed in St. Ludger's Church with thirteen hours of prayer. I went there late in the afternoon[8] and said to myself, 'I'm not leaving here until I have a clearcut assurance whether I may now enter Carmel.' After the concluding blessing had been pronounced, I had the assurance of the Good Shepherd.

That very evening I wrote to Father Archabbot. But he was in Rome, and I did not want to send the letter out of the country. It had to wait in my desk drawer, until I could send it to Beuron. It got to be the middle of May until I received permission to take the preliminary steps in preparation. I did this immediately. Through my catechumen in Cologne[9] I asked Dr. Cosack for an appointment to talk to her. We had met in Aachen in October 1932. She had introduced herself to me because she knew that I felt an inner bond with Carmel and she had told me that she had close ties to the Carmelite Order and especially to the Cologne Carmel. I planned to get information from her concerning the possibilities there. She sent word that the following Sunday (it was Rogation Sunday) or on

---

8   A small tablet now marks this incident of Edith Stein's visit.
9   Hedwig Spiegel, née Hess, who was baptized on August 1, 1933.

Ascension Day she could give me some time. Saturday I received the news in the morning mail. At noon I traveled to Cologne. I telephoned Dr. Cosack, and we agreed that she would pick me up for a walk the following morning.

So far neither she nor my catechumen knew for what purpose I had come. The latter accompanied me to the Carmel for the early morning mass. On the way back, she said to me: "Edith, while I knelt next to you, the thought occurred to me: 'She wouldn't be thinking of entering Carmel now, would she?' " At that point I did not want to keep my secret from her any longer. She promised to keep it confidential. A little bit later, Dr. C. appeared. As soon as we had turned toward the *Stadtwald*, I told her what I had in mind. I immediately added what might be held against me: My age (42), my Jewish descent, my lack of means. She did not consider any of it important. She even held out hopes that I might be accepted here in Cologne, because, due to the founding of a new Carmel in Silesia, vacancies would occur. A new Carmel outside the gates of my hometown Breslau — was that not a sign from heaven? I told Miss Cosack enough about my background for her to form an opinion about my vocation as a Carmelite. She then proposed on her own that we should pay a visit to the Carmel. She was especially close to Sr. Marianne (Countess Praschma)[10], who was to go to Silesia to found the new convent. She would first talk to her.

While she was in the parlor, I knelt in the chapel, close to the altar of little St. Thérèse. I experienced the serenity of someone who has reached her goal. The talk took a long time. When Miss Cosack finally called me, she said confidently, "I believe something will come of it." She had first talked with Sr. Marianne, then with Mother Prioress (at that time M. Josepha of the Blessed Sacrament), and had paved the way for me well. But now the monastic schedule did not allow any more time for the parlor. I was told to return after Vespers. Long before Vespers, I was back in the chapel and participated in the Vesper prayer; after that, May devotions were held behind the choir grille. It was about 3:30 when I was finally called into the parlor. Mother Josepha and our dear mother (Teresia Renata de Spiritu Sancto[11], then subprioress and Mistress of Novices) were

10 A well-known family of nobility in Silesia. Their forebears founded a monastery of Carmelite Brothers in Silesia.

11 Sr. Teresia Renata Posselt, a remarkable woman, was elected Prioress of the Carmel "Maria vom Frieden" in Cologne in 1936. She experienced the destruction of the monastery of Köln-Lindenthal by bombs in October 1944. After World War II she undertook the rebuilding of the monastery on its former site. Mother Renata's biography of Edith Stein, published in 1948, saw many editions and translations. She died in 1961.

at the grille. I explained once more by what road I had reached this point, how the thought of Carmel had never left me; I spent eight years as a teacher with the Dominican nuns in Speyer, was intimately connected with the entire convent, and yet was unable to enter; I considered Beuron the antechamber of heaven, yet it never entered my mind to become a Benedictine nun; it always seemed to me that the Lord was saving something for me in Carmel which I could find there and nowhere else.

That made a deep impression. Mother Teresia had only one hesitation: Could she take responsibility for removing someone from the outside world who could yet accomplish much there? I finally was told to come back when Father Provincial was there. They expected him soon.

That evening I returned to Münster. I had accomplished more than I had expected when I arrived in Cologne. But Father Provincial kept me waiting a long time. During Pentecost I spent most of my time in the Cathedral in Münster. Encouraged by the Holy Spirit, I wrote to Mother Josepha and pleaded urgently for a prompt answer, because in my uncertain situation I had to find out what exactly I had to reckon with. In reply I got an appointment in Cologne. The Vicar for Religious would see me. They (the Nuns) no longer wanted to wait for Father Provincial. This time I was to meet the Chapter nuns who would vote on my admission.

Again I went to Cologne from Saturday afternoon until Sunday night. (I believe it was June 18-19.) I talked to Mother Josepha, Mother Teresia[11] and Sr. Marianne before my visit to Monsignor, and had the opportunity to introduce my friend. On the way to Dr. Lenné, I was caught in a thunderstorm and arrived totally soaked. I had to wait an hour before he appeared. After greeting me, he passed his hand over his forehead and said, "What was that again that you have come to see me about? I have completely forgotten."

I replied that I was applying for admission to Carmel and that I had an appointment with him. Now he knew and stopped asking me questions. I realized later that he had been testing me. I had swallowed it without flinching. He made me repeat everything he already knew, told me what objections he wanted to raise against me, but comforted me with the assurance that the Sisters rarely let his objections deter them and that he usually struck a friendly compromise with them. He then dismissed me with his blessing.

This time, after Vespers, all the Chapter nuns approached the grille. Tiny Sr. Teresia, the community's oldest member, came very close to the grille so as to be able to see and hear clearly. Sr. Aloysia, a liturgy enthusiast, wanted to hear all about Beuron. On that score I could oblige her. Finally I had to sing a song. I had been warned about that the day before, but I had assumed it was a joke. I sang, "Segne Du, Maria," (Bless us, Mary) a bit shyly and softly. Afterwards I said that that had been more difficult for me than addressing a thousand people. As I was to find out later, the Sisters didn't understand that reference, because they did not yet know anything about my activities as a lecturer. After the Sisters had withdrawn, Mother Josepha told me that the vote could not take place until next morning. Thus I had to leave that night without knowing. Sr. Marianne, to whom I talked privately at the end, promised to notify me by telegram. And indeed, the next day, the telegram arrived. "Joyful assent. Regards, Carmel." I read it and went into the chapel to give thanks.

We had already made plans. By July 15 I wanted to wind up everything in Münster, and on the 16th I planned to take part in celebrating the Feast of the Queen of Carmel (with the Sisters in Cologne). After that I was to live for one month as a guest in the extern quarters. In mid-August I would travel home on a round trip ticket and be admitted into the enclosure on October 15 for the Feast of our Holy Mother. Beyond that it was planned to transfer me later to the Silesian Carmel.

Six large cartons of books traveled to Cologne ahead of me. I had written to them that it was not likely that any other Carmelite had brought such a dowry with her. Sr. Ursula took them under her care and took great pains to keep theology, philosophy, philology, etc. apart. (This was the way the boxes were labeled.) But in the end, everything got mixed up.

Few people in Münster knew where I was going. I wanted to keep it as secret as possible as long as my family was not informed. Among the few who knew was the Mother Superior of the Marianum. I had confided in her as soon as the telegram came. She had worried about me a great deal and was very glad now. Shortly before my departure, a farewell gathering was held in the music room of the house. The women students had prepared it with much affection, and the nuns took part as well. I thanked them briefly and told them that later, when they would find out where I had gone, they would rejoice with me. The Sisters of the Order gave me a cross, a relic which the late Bishop Johannes von Poggenburg[12] had given them. Sr. Prioress brought it to me on a paten, covered with roses.

---

12 Johannes v. Poggenburg, 1862—1933, Bishop of Münster from 1913 to 1933. This cross is at present in the *Edith-Stein-Archiv,* Carmel "Maria vom Frieden," Cologne. Edith Stein gave it to her friend Hedwig Spiegel (See Footnote # 9) on the occasion of her baptism. Mrs. Spiegel left it to the Cologne Carmel in her will. It was used in the Beatification Ceremony, May 1, 1987.

Five students and the librarian of the Institute accompanied me to the train station. I was able to take huge bouquets of roses along for the Feast of the Queen of Carmel. Less than eighteen months earlier, I had gone to Münster a stranger. Aside from my professional activities, I had lived in monastic seclusion. Nevertheless I now left a large circle of people who were bound to me in love and loyalty. I have always held the beautiful old town and the Münster countryside in fond and grateful memory.

To my family I had only written that I had found a place to stay in Cologne with a group of nuns and would move there for good in October. They wished me good luck as one would for a new job.

The month in the extern quarters was a very happy time. I took part in the entire daily routine, worked during the hours outside of prayers, and was allowed into the parlor now and then. All questions that came up I submitted to Mother Josepha; her decision always coincided with what I would have done on my own. This inner agreement made me very happy.

My catechumen came to see me often. She wanted to be baptized before my departure, so that I could be her godmother. On August 1, Prelate Lenné[13] baptized her in the Cathedral Chapter Room, and the following morning she received her first holy communion in the convent chapel. Her husband was present at both celebrations, but he could not make up his mind to follow her example. On August 10, I met Father Archabbot in Trier and received his blessing for the difficult journey to Breslau. I contemplated the Holy Robe (of Trier)[14] and prayed for strength. I also knelt for a long time at the shrine in St. Matthew's Church, where many favors had been granted. That night I found hospitality at Cordel[15], where our dear Mother Teresia Renata had been Mistress of Novices for nine years, until she was called back to Cologne as subprioress. On August 14, my godchild and I went to Maria Laach for the Feast of Our Lady's Assumption. From there I continued on to Breslau.

13 Lenné, Albert, born 1878 Strassburg, died 1958 Cologne.

14 The Holy Robe is an ancient, seamless garment purported to be the robe worn by Jesus of Nazareth. After the crucifixion, the Roman soldiers drew lots to decide who should get it. Bloody battles have been fought over it, though its authenticity is at best doubtful. It has been the object of veneration over the centuries and is carefully preserved in a chapel in the Cathedral of Trier and occasionally on view to the faithful. Because the garment is all of one piece, it assumes a symbolic significance, standing for unity not only of all Christians, but also of the nations of the world.

15 Small town on the Moselle River, now spelled Kordel. Because of almost constant flood conditions, the Kordel Carmel has been moved to Anderath-Waldfrieden.

At the train station, my sister Rosa was waiting for me. Since she had felt herself a part of the Church for a long time and was in full agreement with me, I told her right away what my plans were. She showed no surprise, and yet I noticed that not even she had had an inkling of it. The others asked no questions at all for about two to three weeks. Only my nephew Wolfgang (then twenty-one years old) inquired immediately, as soon as he came to welcome me, what I was going to do in Cologne. I answered him honestly but asked him to keep it confidential for now.

My mother suffered greatly under the political conditions. She became upset again and again over the fact that "there are such wicked people in the world." Added to that there was a personal loss which affected her badly. My sister Erna was to take over the medical practice of our friend Lilli Berg who was going to Palestine with her family. The Bibersteins[16] had to move into the Bergs' apartment in the south of the city and leave our house. Erna and her two children were a comfort and joy to my mother. Having to miss her daily contact with them was very bitter for her. But despite all these depressing concerns, she revived when I came. Her cheerfulness and her humor came through once again.

When she got home from work, she liked to sit down next to my desk with her knitting and to talk about all her domestic and business worries. I also let her tell me again her reminiscences of the past, as a foundation for a family history which I started at that time. This cozy togetherness was really good for her. As for me, I kept thinking: If only you knew!

It was a great comfort to me that at that time Sr. Marianne was in Breslau with her cousin Sr. Elisabeth (Countess Stolberg), in order to prepare for the founding of the new convent. They had left Cologne for Breslau prior to me. Sr. Marianne had visited my mother and brought her my regards. During my stay in Breslau, she came to our house twice more and became quite friendly with my mother. When I visited her at the Ursuline convent where she lived, I could speak freely and vent my true feelings. On the other hand, I was told about all the joys and troubles of the founding of the convent, and once was allowed to accompany the two sisters to the construction site in Pawelwitz (now Wendelborn).

I helped Erna a lot with the move. During a trolley ride to the new apartment, she finally put the question about the situation in Cologne. When I answered, she grew pale, and there were tears in her eyes.

16 Erna, Edith's sister, was married to Dr. Hans Biberstein.

24

Auguste Stein (nee Courant), mother of Edith Stein.

"How dreadful life is!" she said, "What makes one person happy is for another the worst blow imaginable."

She did not try to dissuade me. A few days later she told me on behalf of her husband that, if worry about my livelihood were a contributing factor in my decision, then I should know that I could live with them as long as they still had anything. (My brother-in-law in Hamburg had said the same thing.) Erna added that she was obliged to give me this message, even though she knew very well that such reasons would carry no weight with me.

On the first Sunday in September, my mother and I were alone in the house. She was sitting at the window knitting a sock. I sat close by. All of a sudden came the long-expected question:

"What will you do with the Sisters in Cologne?"

"Live with them."

Now there followed a desperate denial. My mother never stopped knitting. Her yarn became tangled; with trembling hands she sought to unravel it, and I helped her as our discussion continued.

From now on all tranquility had vanished. A cloud lay upon the entire household. From time to time, my mother attempted a new assault. Quiet desperation would follow. My niece Erika, the most observant Jew in the family, felt an obligation to influence me. My brothers and sisters did not try, since they considered it useless. It got even worse when my sister Else arrived from Hamburg for Mother's birthday. While my mother usually controlled her emotions firmly when she was with me, she got very upset in talking to Else. My sister related to me all these outbursts, because she thought that I was unaware of how my mother felt.

Aside from this, the family experienced severe economic problems. The business had been doing very badly for some time. Now *that* half of the house which the Bibersteins had inhabited, stood empty. People came to look at it every day, but no deal was ever concluded. Among the most eager aspirants was a Protestant congregation. One day when, once again, three of their clergymen appeared, my mother asked me to go with them to the empty apartment; she was already sick of it.

I managed to get to the point at which we formulated all conditions. I reported back to my mother and in her behalf wrote to the head pastor[17] asking for his written assent. Indeed it was given. Nevertheless the entire affair threatened to come undone shortly

17 A recent article by historian Franz Heiduk of Würzburg, formerly a resident of Silesia, explores the identity of this "head pastor" and concludes that it must have been Stadtdekan Walther Lierse. For Heiduk's interesting thesis see *Schlesien* v. 33, 1988, p. 129-135.

before my departure. I wanted to take at least this worry off my mother's shoulders and therefore called upon the gentleman in his place of residence. It seemed hopeless, but when I turned to go, he said, "Now you look so sad. I'm sorry."

I told him that my mother had so many worries at this time. He asked me compassionately, what kind of worries these were. I spoke briefly about my conversion and my monastic plans. That made a big impression.

"I want you to know before you go there, that you have won a sympathetic heart here."

He called his wife, and after some deliberations they decided to call another board meeting and to bring the matter up once more. And before my departure, the head pastor came to our house with his colleagues to conclude the deal. In parting he whispered to me "God bless you."

Sr. Marianne had another private talk with my mother. It accomplished little. Sr. Marianne was not willing to try to deter me (as my mother hoped). And any other consolation was unacceptable. Of course (while they refused to dissuade me) the two sisters would not have presumed to reinforce my decision further by their encouragement. The decision was so difficult that no one could tell me with certainty which was the right path. Good reasons could be cited for both alternatives. I had to take that step in the complete darkness of faith. During those weeks I often thought: Which of us two will break down, my mother or I? But both of us managed to persevere to the last day.

Shortly before my departure I had a dental checkup. While I sat in the dentist's waiting room, the door opened and my niece Susel entered. She blushed with pleasure. Unbeknownst to us, both our appointments had been made for the same time. We both went into the office, and afterwards she accompanied me home. She hung on my arm, and I took the child's brown hand in mine. Susel was twelve years old at that time, but mature and thoughtful beyond her years. I had never been permitted to talk to the children about my conversion, but by now Erna had told them everything; for this I was grateful.

I asked the child to visit Grandmother often after I was gone. She promised to do so.

"Why are you doing this *now?*" she asked.

I understood very clearly what kind of parental discussions she had witnessed. I gave her my reasons as if she were an adult. She listened thoughtfully and understood.

Two days before my departure, her father (Hans Biberstein) came to see me. He felt obliged to state his objections even though he saw no hope for success. What I was planning appeared to him to draw the line between myself and the Jewish people more sharply than before, and that just now, when they were so sorely oppressed. The fact that I saw it very differently he could not understand.

My last day at home was October 12, my birthday. It coincided with a Jewish holiday, the end of the Feast of Tabernacles. My mother attended services in the synagogue of the rabbinical seminary. I accompanied her, because we wanted to spend as much of this day together as possible. Erika's favorite teacher, an eminent scholar, gave a beautiful sermon. On the way there on the trolley we had not talked very much. In order to comfort her a little, I had said that at first there would be a probationary period. But that was no help.

"If you take on a probationary period, I know that you will pass."

Now my mother asked to walk home, a distance of about forty-five minutes, and this at eighty-four years of age! But I had to consent, for I knew well that she wanted to talk with me undisturbed a little longer.

"Wasn't it a beautiful sermon?"

"Yes, it was."

"It's possible then to be devout as a Jew also?"

"Certainly, if one has not come to know anything else."

Now she replied, sounding desperate: "Why did you have to come to know it? I don't want to say anything against *him*. He may have been a very good man. But why did he make himself into God?"

After lunch she went to the office, so that my sister Frieda would not be left alone during my brother's lunch time. But she told me she would come back soon, and she did (solely for my sake; on other days she still spent all day at work).

Many visitors came that afternoon and evening; all the brothers and sisters, their children, my women friends. That was good, because it was distracting. But as one after another said good-bye and left, it became difficult. Finally my mother and I were left alone in the room. My sisters were still busy with dishwashing and cleanup. Then she covered her face with her hands and began to weep. I stood behind her chair and held her silvery head to my breast. Thus we remained for a long while, until she let me persuade her to go to bed. I took her upstairs and helped her undress, for the first time in my life. Then I sat on the edge of her bed till she herself sent me to bed. . . I don't think either of us found any rest that night.

My train was due to leave at about 8 a.m. Else and Rosa wanted to accompany me to the station. Erna had also wanted to come, but I begged her to come to the house early instead and stay with my mother. I knew that she would be best able to calm her. We two youngest ones had always retained our childhood tenderness toward Mother. The older siblings were embarrassed by it, even though they surely did not love her any less. At half past five I left the house as usual to attend early mass in St. Michael's Church. Afterwards we gathered around the breakfast table. Erna arrived about 7 o'clock. My mother tried to eat something, but soon she pushed her cup aside and began to cry as on the previous night.

I returned to her and put my arms around her until it was time to go. I motioned to Erna to take my place. I put on hat and coat next door; then came the good-bye. My mother embraced and kissed me warmly. Erika thanked me for all my help. (I had helped her prepare for her exam as a middle school teacher; as I was packing, she still kept coming to me with questions.) In the end she added, "May the Eternal be with you." When I embraced Erna, my mother wept aloud. I left quickly; Rosa and Else followed. When the trolley on which we were riding passed our house, there was no one at the window as on other occasions to wave a last farewell.

At the station we had to wait a short while for the train to arrive. Else clung to me. After I had saved a seat for myself, I went to the window and looked down at my sisters. I was struck by the difference in the two faces. Rosa was so serene as if she were going along into the tranquility of the convent. Else on the other hand, in her grief suddenly resembled an old woman.

Finally the train began to move. Both waved as long as we could get even a glimpse of each other. At last they left. I could now withdraw to my seat in the compartment. So what I had scarcely yet hoped for would now become reality. I could not feel any wild joy. The scene I had just left behind was too terrible for that. But I felt a deep peace, in the harbor of the divine will.

I arrived in Cologne late at night. My godchild had asked me to spend one more night at their house. I was not supposed to be received within the enclosure until the next day after Vespers.

In the morning I announced my arrival at the convent and was permitted to come to the grille for a welcome. Soon after lunch we were back again to attend Vespers in the chapel; First Vespers of the Feast of our Holy Mother. Earlier, while kneeling in the sanctuary, I heard someone whisper at the sacristy turn: "Is Edith outside?"

Then a bunch of big white chrysanthemums was delivered to me. Teachers from the Palatinate had sent them in welcome. I was supposed to see the flowers before they were used to decorate the altar.

After Vespers we were asked to have coffee. Then a lady arrived, who introduced herself as the sister of our dear Mother Teresia Renata. She asked which one of us was the postulant; she wanted to offer some encouragement. But there was no need of that. This sponsor and my godchild accompanied me to the door of the enclosure. At last it opened, and in deep peace I crossed the threshold into the House of the Lord.

Home of Auguste Stein, Michaelis St. 38, Wroclaw (formerly Breslau). At the windows on the upper floor are Susanne and Ernst Ludwig Biberstein (niece and nephew of Edith Stein) with their paternal grandmother, Dorothea Biberstein. At the next window to the right is Dr. Erna Biberstein (nee Stein), the sister of Edith. Susanne is the editor and translator of this book.

Poems and Prayers

Selected and Introduced by
Waltraud Herbstrith
(Teresia a Matre Dei OCD)

Edith Stein in passport photo taken in December, 1938, just before leaving for Echt, Netherlands.

Introduction

by Waltraud Herbstrith (Teresia a Matre Dei OCD) editor of the original German edition.

With these simple prayers Edith Stein confronts us, not as a profound philosopher or superior correspondent. These words or stanzas could be anyone's, those of a simple Christian who expresses his joys and sorrows in artless language. That is what surprises us, that Edith Stein, despite her intellectual ability and extensive education could be uncomplicated and carefree as a child. Abbot Raphael Walzer of Beuron gave testimony that her piety was simple and down-to-earth. To some who expect great literary sophistication of her, even in her prayers, this is a disappointment.

Edith Stein rarely discussed her religious feelings and ideas. During the last nine years of her life, in the Carmelite monasteries of Cologne and Echt, she had been asked on several occasions to compose brief texts for special occasions. That is how these words reached us. As her point of departure, Edith Stein nearly always took a word from Scripture, which she adapted in simple form and versified, often too hastily for our taste. What impresses us in these lines is the atmosphere of depth, of peace, of childlike trust in God. Her preoccupation with judgment and retribution was obviously due to the horrible destruction of the Jewish people. Yet her trust in God's unfathomable mercy never falters. Edith Stein's piety was nourished by the psalms, the celebration of the Eucharist, and by her delving into the passion of Jesus Christ on the Mount of Olives and the jubilant gladness which the Divine Spirit grants us. Despite all darkness and depression, the light of God, God's love, is finally victorious. That is the triumphant joy which Edith passes along to those who pray with her.

Meinem Herzen entströmt festlicher Sang:
Ich weihe mein Lied dem König.

Psalm 45:1

1. Aus mei - nem Her - zen strömt die
   Es will die Zun - ge ihm zum

Wei - se: Ich will mein Lied dem Kö - nig weihn.
Prei - se des Schrei-bers schnel- le Fe - der sein.

Gar herr - lich ist er von Ge - stalt

und sieg - reich sei - nes Arms Ge - walt.

2. Ihm steht die Königin zur Seite in goldgeschmücktem Prachtge-
wand; ihr geben Jungfraun das Geleite, die er berief zu hohem
Stand. Ein Jubelchor, so gehn sie hin, ins Haus des Königs ein-
zuziehn.

Weise: Adolf Lohmann

36

My heart is stirred by a noble theme;
I address my poem to the king.

Psalm 45:1

1. A festive song streams from my heart,
   Which to the King I dedicate
   My tongue shall take the pen's swift part
   His praises duly to relate.
   He is most glorious to behold
   His arm is powerful and bold.

2. The Queen stands ever by His side
   In splendid, gold-brocaded gown;
   Demure young maidens with her stride
   Whom He has raised to high renown.
   A joyous chorus, sweet they sing,
   Ent'ring the palace of the King.

Melody: Adolf Lohmann

Edith Stein wrote the poem on the following page near the start of her life as a Carmelite, probably in 1934 or 1935, for a festival. The poem refers to the novitiate and the role played by the Mistress of Novices and the Prioress. In a prayer in use at that time and still used in many Carmelite monasteries today, Teresa of Avila is compared to a planter and guardian of vineyards, using the metaphor which occurs in the *Song of Songs*.

Früh zu den Weinbergen lass uns ausgehen
und sehen, ob die Reben treiben.

Hld 7, 13.

KARMELWEINBERG

Melodie: Segne, o Maria.

Lass uns, mein Geliebter,
in den Weinberg gehn!
Komm, am frühen Morgen
wollen still wir sehn,
ob der Weinberg blühet,
ob er Früchte treibt,
ob das Leben glühet,
frisch die Rebe bleibt.

Komm' aus Himmelshöhen,
heil'ge Mutter Du,
führe Deinem Weinberg
den Geliebten zu.
Tau und Regen spende
seine milde Hand,
warme Sonne sende
Er dem Karmelland.

Auch den kleinsten Reben,
neu erst eingesenkt,
werde Himmelsleben
gnadenvoll geschenkt.
Treue Winzer stützen
ihre schwache Kraft,
vor dem Feind sie schützen,
der im Dunkeln schafft.

Heil'ge Mutter, lohne
Deiner Winzer Müh'.
Mit der Himmelskrone
einst erwarte sie.
Keine dieser Reben
gib dem Feuer preis,
führ' zum ew'gen Leben
jedes junge Reis.

In the morning we will go to the vineyards.
We will see if the vines are budding.

Song of Songs 7:13

VINEYARD OF CARMEL

Come, love, to the vineyard
In the morning dew,
There we'll watch in silence,
If vineyards bloom anew,
If the grapes are growing,
Life with vigor glowing,
Fresh the vine and true.

From the heights of Heaven
Holy Mother descend,
Lead unto your vineyard
Our beloved friend.
Dew and rain let gently
Drop from His kind hand
And the balm of sunshine
Fall on Carmel's land.

Young vines, newly planted,
Tiny though they be,
Grant them life eternal
A gift of grace from Thee.
Trusted vintners strengthen
Their frail and feeble powers,
Shield them from the enemy
Who in darkness cowers.

Holy Mother grant reward
For your vintners' care
Give them, I beseech you
Crown of Heaven fair.
Don't let raging fire
Kill these vines, we pray,
And grant your life eternal
To each young shoot some day.

The following poem was written for the Feast of Corpus Christi, probably in 1935. On that date, Sister Maria, nee Ernst, took her vows. She had entered Carmel shortly after Edith. This text is preserved in booklet form, adorned with small pen drawings. It is likely that it was presented to the celebrant. The English translation begins on page 49.

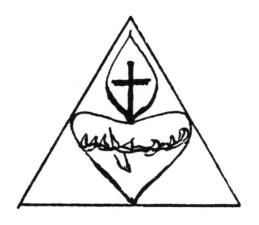

„Ich bleibe bei Euch ..."

Du thronest an des Vaters rechter Hand
Im Reiche seiner ew'gen Herrlichkeit
Als Gottes Wort von Anbeginn.
Du herrschest auf dem allerhöchsten
Auch in verklärter menschlicher Ge-
                                    Thron
                                    stalt,
Seitdem vollbracht Dein
        Erdenwerk.
So glaube ich, weil es Dein Wort
                    mich lehrt,
Und weil ich glaube, weiß ich es
                    beglückt,
Und sel'ge Hoffnung draus
        erblüht:
Denn wo Du bist, da sind die
                    Deinen auch,
Der Himmel ist mein herrlich
                    Vaterland,
Ich teil' mit Dir des Vaters
        Thron.

2.

Der Ewige, der alle Wesen schuf,
Der, dreimal heilig, alles Sein
umfaßt,
Hat noch ein eig'nes stilles
Reich.

Der Menschenseele innerstes Gemach
Ist des Dreifalt'gen liebster Aufent-
halt,
Sein Himmelsthron im Erdenland.

Dies Himmelreich aus Feindeshand
zu lösen,
Ist Gottes Sohn als Menschensohn
gekommen,
Er gab sein Blut als Lösepreis.

Im Herzen Jesu, das durchstochen
ward,
Sind Himmelreich und Erdenland
verbunden,
Hier ist für uns des Lebens
Quell.

Dies Herz ist der Dreifalt'gen Gottheit
Herz
Und aller Menschenherzen Mittelpunkt,
Das uns der Gottheit Leben
spendet.

Es zieht uns an sich mit geheimer
Macht,
Es birgt in sich uns in des Vaters
Schoß
Und strömt uns zu dem
Heil'gen Geist.
Dies Herz, es schlägt für uns im
kleinen Zelt,
Wo es geheimnisvoll verborgen weilt,
In jenem stillen, weißen Rund.

Das ist Dein Königsthron, o Herr, auf
Erden,
Den sichtbar Du für uns errichtet hast
Und gerne siehst Du mich
ihm nah'n.

Du senkest voll Liebe Deinen Blick,
        in meinen
Und neigst Dein Ohr zu meinen
        leisen Worten
Und füllst mit Frieden tief
        das Herz.

Doch Deine Liebe findet kein Ge-
        nügen
In diesem Austausch, der noch
        Trennung läßt:
Dein Herz verlangt nach mehr.

Du kommst als Frühmahl zu mir
        jeden Morgen,
Dein Fleisch und Blut wird mir
        zu Trank und Speise
Und Wunderbares wird gewirkt.

Dein Leib durchdringt geheimnisvoll
        den meinen,
Und Deine Seele eint sich mit der
        meinen:
Ich bin nicht mehr, was einst
        ich war.

Du kommst und gehst, doch bleibt
          zurück die Saat,
Die Du gesät zu künft'ger Herrlichkeit
Verborgen in dem Leib von Staub.

Es bleibt ein Glanz des Himmels in
          der Seele,
Es bleibt ein tiefes Leuchten in den
                    Augen,
Ein Schweben in der Stimme Klang.

Es bleibt das Band, das Herz
          mit Herz verbindet,
Der Lebensstrom, der aus dem
          Deinen quillt
Und jedes Glied belebt.
          *
Wie wunderbar sind Deiner Liebe
                    Wunder,
Wir staunen nur und stammeln
          und verstummen,
Weil Blick und Wort
     * versagt *
          *

Clothing ceremony, April 15, 1934 shows Edith as Sister Teresa Benedicta in her bridal gown of white silk.

Wer mein Fleisch isst und mein Blut trinkt, bleibt
in mir und ich in ihm. Wie mich der lebendige Vater
gesandt hat und ich durch den Vater lebe, so wird
auch der, der mich isst, durch mich leben.

Joh 6, 56/7

"ICH BLEIBE BEI EUCH. . ."

Du thronest an des Vaters rechter Hand
Im Reiche seiner ew'gen Herrlichkeit
Als Gottes Wort von Anbeginn.

Du herrschest auf dem allerhöchsten Thron
Auch in verklärter menschlicher Gestalt,
Seitdem vollbracht Dein Erdenwerk.

So glaube ich, weil es Dein Wort mich lehrt,
Und weil ich glaube, weiss ich es beglückt,
Und sel'ge Hoffnung draus erblüht:

Denn wo Du bist, da sind die Deinen auch,
Der Himmel ist mein herrlich Vaterland,
Ich teil' mit Dir des Vaters Thron.

Der Ewige, der alle Wesen schuf,
Der, dreimal heilig, alles Sein umfasst,
Hat noch ein eig'nes stilles Reich.

Der Menschenseele innerstes Gemach
Ist des Dreifalt'gen liebster Aufenthalt,
Sein Himmelsthron im Erdenland.

Dies Himmelreich aus Feindeshand zu lösen,
Ist Gottes Sohn als Menschensohn gekommen,
Er gab sein Blut als Lösepreis.

Im Herzen Jesu, das durchstochen ward,
Sind Himmelreich und Erdenland verbunden,
Hier ist für uns des Lebens Quell.

He who eats my flesh and drinks my blood
lives in me
and I live in him.
As I, who am sent by the living Father
myself draw life from the Father.
So who ever eats me will draw life from me.

John 6:56-57

"I SHALL STAY WITH YOU. . ."

Your throne is at the Lord's right hand,
Within the realm of His eternal glory,
God's word from when the world began.

You reign upon the highest throne of all,
Even in transfigured human form,
Since you fulfilled your task on earth.

So I believe, because your word has taught me,
And, thus believing, know that this delights me,
And blessed hope blooms out of it.

For where you are, there also are your dear ones.
And Heaven is my glorious fatherland,
With you I share the Father's throne.

The Eternal One, creator of all being,
Who, holy thrice, encompasses all life,
Retains a quiet realm all to Himself.

The inmost chamber of the human soul
Is favorite dwelling to the Trinity,
His heavenly throne right here on earth.

To free this heav'nly realm from hostile hand,
God's Son descended as the Son of Man.
He gave His blood as ransom.

Within the heart of Jesus pierced with lances,
The realms of heaven and earth become united.
And here we find the spring of life itself.

Dies Herz ist der Dreifalt'gen Gottheit Herz
Und aller Menschenherzen Mittelpunkt,
Das uns der Gottheit Leben spendet.

Es zieht uns an sich mit geheimer Macht,
Es birgt in sich uns in des Vaters Schoss
Und strömt uns zu den Heil'gen Geist.

Dies Herz, es schlägt für uns im kleinen Zelt,
Wo es geheimnisvoll verborgen weilt
In jenem stillen weissen Rund.

Das ist Dein Königsthron, o Herr, auf Erden,
Den sichtbar Du für uns errichtet hast,
Und gerne siehst Du mich ihm nah'n.

Du senkst voll Liebe Deinen Blick in meinen
Und neigst Dein Ohr zu meinen leisen Worten
Und füllst mit Frieden tief das Herz.

Doch Deine Liebe findet kein Genügen
In diesem Austausch, der noch Trennung lässt:
Dein Herz verlangt nach mehr.

Du kommst als Frühmahl zu mir jeden Morgen,
Dein Fleisch und Blut wird mir zu Trank und Speise
Und Wunderbares wird gewirkt.

Dein Leib durchdringt geheimnisvoll den meinen,
Und Deine Seele eint sich mit der meinen:
Ich bin nicht mehr, was einst ich war.

Du kommst und gehst, doch bleibt zurück die Saat,
Die Du gesät zu künft'ger Herrlichkeit
Verborgen in dem Leib von Staub.

Es bleibt ein Glanz des Himmels in der Seele,
Es bleibt ein tiefes Leuchten in den Augen,
Ein Schweben in der Stimme Klang.

Es bleibt das Band, das Herz mit Herz verbindet,
Der Lebensstrom, der aus dem Deinen quillt
Und jedes Glied belebt.

This is the heart of Trinity divine,
The center also of all human hearts.
Source of our life from God.

It draws us close with its mysterious might,
It keeps us safe within the Father's lap
And floods us with the Holy Spirit.

This heart beats in a tiny tabernacle
Where it remains in hidden mystery,
Within that orbit, silent, white.

That is Your royal throne, O Lord, on earth,
Which You have built for us, plainly to see.
It pleases you when I draw near.

Your eyes look deeply into mine with love,
And to my whispered words You bend Your ear.
You fill my heart with deepest peace.

And yet Your love cannot be satisfied
By this exchange, for there remains a gap,
Your heart still asks for more.

Each morn you come to me as early Mass,
Your flesh and blood become my food and drink;
And wonders are accomplished.

Your body permeates mine mysteriously,
I feel Your soul becoming one with mine:
I am no longer what I used to be.

You come and go, but still the seed remains
Which You have sown for future splendor,
Hid in the body made from dust.

A heavenly radiance lingers in the soul,
And deeply shines a light within the eye,
A vibrant music in the voice.

The tie remains connecting heart to heart,
The stream of life which wells from Yours and gives
Life to each limb.

Wie wunderbar sind Deiner Liebe Wunder,
Wir staunen nur und stammeln und verstummen,
Weil Geist und Wort versagt.

How wondrous are the marvels of your love,
We are amazed, we stammer and grow dumb,
For word and spirit fail us.

Rosa and Edith in a photo taken in Echt, Netherlands, where Edith had been transferred Dec. 31, 1938 and where Rosa joined her on July 1, 1939 as portress at the monastery. Both sisters were arrested on August 2, 1942 and killed in Auschwitz probably on August 9.

Rosa Stein (1883—1942) was an older sister of Edith, who became a Roman Catholic after the death of their mother. The original text of the following poem, donated by Sister Johanna of Beek, Holland, later of Echt, is now in the Edith-Stein-Archiv, Carmel "Maria vom Frieden." The English translation begins on page 59.

Zu Rosa's Taufe

Heilige Nacht.

(Zur Erinnerung an den 24. XII. 36)

Mein Herr und Gott,
Du hast mich einen langen,
dunklen Weg geführt,
schwüg und hart.

Oft wollten meine Kräfte mir versagen,
Fast hofft' ich nimmer, je das Licht zu schau'n.
Doch als in tiefstem Schmerz mein Herz erstarrt,
Da ging ein klarer, milder Stern mir auf.
Er führte mich getreu – ich folgt' ihm,
Zagend erst, dann immer sicher vor.
So stand ich endlich an dem Tor der Kirche.

Es tat sich auf – ich bat um Einlaß.
Aus Deines Priesters Mund grüßt mich Dein Segenswort.
Im Innern reiht sich Stern auf Stern.
Rote Blütensterne weisen mir den Weg zu Dir.
Sie harren Dein zur Heil'gen Nacht.
Doch Deine Güte
Läßt sie mir leuchten auf dem Weg zu Dir.
Sie führen mich voran.
Das Geheimnis, das ich im Herzen tief verborgen mußte,
Nun darf ich laut es künden:
Ich glaube – ich bekenne!

56

Der Priester geleitet mich die Stufen zum Altar
hinauf:
Ich neige die Stirn —
Das heil'ge Wasser fließt mir übers
Haupt.

— — — —

Ist's möglich Herr, daß einer neu geboren wird,
Der schon des Lebens Mitte überschritten?
Du hast's gesagt, und mir ward's Wirklichkeit
Eines langen Lebens Last an Schuld und Leiden
Fiel von mir.
Angsterlöst empfang' ich den weißen Mantel,

Den sie mir um die Schultern legen,
Der Reinheit lichtes Bild!
Ich trag in meiner Hand die Kerze.
Ihre Flamme zündet,
Daß in mir Dein heil'ges Leben glüht.
Mein Herz ist nun zur Krippe worden,
Die Deiner harrt.
Nicht lange!
Maria, Deine und auch meine Mutter
Hat schon Namen mir gegeben.
Um Mitternacht legt sie ihr neugebor'nes Kind
Mir in das Herz.
O, keines Menschen Herz vermag's zu fassen,
Was denn Du bereitest, die Dich lieben.
Nun hab ich Dich und lasse Dich nimmermehr,
Wo immer meines Lebens Schiffe geht,
Nichts kann von Deinem Bilde ...

Fürchtet euch nicht! Denn siehe, ich verkünde euch
eine große Freude. . . Herrlichkeit in den Höhen für
Gott und auf Erden Friede den Menschen seiner
Huld!

Lk 2,10.14

ZU ROSA'S TAUFE.
HEILIGE NACHT.
(Zur Erinnerung an den 24. XII.36)

Mein Herr und Gott,
Du hast mich einen langen, dunklen Weg geführt,
Steinig und hart.
Oft wollten meine Kräfte mir versagen,
Fast hofft' ich nimmer, je das Licht zu schau'n.
Doch als im tiefsten Schmerz mein Herz erstarrte,
Da ging ein klarer, milder Stern mir auf.
Er führte mich getreu—ich folgt' ihm,
Zagend zuerst, dann immer sich'rer.
So stand ich endlich an dem Tor der Kirche.
Es tat sich auf—ich bat um Einlass.
Aus Deines Priesters Mund grüsst mich Dein Segenswort.
Im Innern reiht sich Stern an Stern.
Rote Blütensterne weisen mir den Weg zu Dir.
Sie harren Dein zur heil'gen Nacht,
Doch Deine Güte
Lässt sie mir leuchten auf dem Weg zu Dir.
Sie führen mich voran.
Das Geheimnis, das ich im Herzen tief verbergen musste,
Nun darf ich laut es künden:
Ich glaube—ich bekenne!
Der Priester geleitet mich die Stufen zum Altar hinauf:
Ich neige die Stirn —
Das heil'ge Wasser fliesst mir übers Haupt.

"Do not be afraid. Listen, I bring you news of great joy,
a joy to be shared by the whole people. . . Glory to God in the
highest heaven, and peace to men who enjoy his favor."

Luke 2:10,14

FOR ROSA'S BAPTISM.
HOLY NIGHT,
(In remembrance of December 24, 1936.)

My Lord, God,
You have led me by a long, dark path,
Rocky and hard.
Often my strength threatened to fail me.
I almost lost all hope of seeing the light.
But when my heart grew numb with deepest grief,
A clear star rose for me.
Steadfast it guided me—I followed,
At first reluctant, but more confidently later.

At last I stood at Church's gate.
It opened. I sought admission.
From Your priest's mouth Your blessing greets me.
Within me stars are strung like pearls.
Red blossom stars show me the path to You.
They wait for you at Holy Night.
But your goodness
Allows them to illuminate my path to You.
They lead me on.
The secret which I had to keep in hiding
Deep in my heart,
Now I can shout it out:
I believe—I profess!
The priest accompanies me to the altar:
I bend my face—
Holy water flows over my head

Ist's möglich, Herr, dass einer neu geboren wird,
Der schon des Lebens Mitte überschritten?
Du hast's gesagt, und mir ward's Wirklichkeit.
Eines langen Lebens Last an Schuld und Leiden
Fiel von mir.
Aufrecht empfang' ich den weissen Mantel,
Den sie mir um die Schultern legen,
Der Reinheit lichtes Bild!
Ich trag in meiner Hand die Kerze,
Ihre Flamme kündet,
Dass in mir Dein heil'ges Leben glüht.

Mein Herz ist nun zur Krippe worden,
Die Deiner harrt.
Nicht lange!
Maria, Deine und auch meine Mutter
Hat ihren Namen mir gegeben.
Um Mitternacht legt sie ihr neugebor'nes Kind
Mir in das Herz.

O, keines Menschen Herz vermag's zu fassen,
Was denen Du bereitest, die Dich lieben.
Nun hab ich Dich und lass Dich nimmermehr.
Wo immer meines Lebens Strasse geht,
Bist Du bei mir,
Nichts kann von Deiner Liebe je mich scheiden.

Lord, is it possible that someone who is past
Midlife can be reborn?
You said so, and for me it was fulfilled,
A long life's burden of guilt and suffering
Fell away from me.
Erect I receive the white cloak,
Which they place round my shoulders,
Radiant image of purity!
In my hand I hold a candle.
Its flame makes known
That deep within me glows Your holy life.

My heart has become Your manger,
Awaiting You,
But not for long!
Maria, Your mother and also mine
Has given me her name.
At midnight she will place her newborn child
Into my heart.

Ah, no one's heart can fathom,
What You've in store for those who love You.
Now You are mine, and I won't let You go.
Wherever my life's road may lead,
You are with me.
Nothing can ever part me from Your love.

Höre mein Rufen, o Gott. . .
Ich rufe zu dir vom Ende der Erde.

Psalm 61

1. Er - hör, o Gott, mein Fle - hen, hab auf mein
Be - ten acht! Du sahst von fern mich ste - hen, ich
rief aus dunk - ler Nacht. Auf ei - nes Fel - sens
Hö - he er - heb mich gnä - dig - lich! Auf
dich ich hoffend se - he: du lenkst und lei - test mich.

2. Du bist gleich einem Turme, den nie der Feind be-
zwang. Ich weiche keinem Sturme, bei dir ist mir nicht
bang. In deinem Zelt bewahren willst du mich immerdar.
Mich hütet vor Gefahren dein schirmend Flügelpaar.

3. Mein Bitten hast erhöret, mein Gott, in Gnaden du.
Wer deinen Namen ehret, dem fällt dein Erbe zu. So schen-
ke langes Leben dem, der sich dir geweiht, wollst Jahr
um Jahr ihm geben, ihn segnen allezeit!

4. Vor Gottes Angesichte steh er in Ewigkeit! Es wird
ja nie zunichte des Herrn Barmherzigkeit. — So will dein
Lied ich singen, wie ich es dir versprach, mein Lobesopfer
bringen von neuem Tag um Tag!

Weise: Französischer Psalter, Lyon 1547

62

God, hear my cry for help,
    listen to my prayer!
From the ends of the earth I call to you.

Psalm 61:1-2

1.   God, hear me, I implore You,
    And listen to my prayer.
    You saw me stand before You
    In darkness and despair.
    O lift me, gracious Ruler,
    Upon a rocky peak.
    With hope I look to You, God,
    Your guiding hand I seek.

2.   You are a sturdy tower
    Resisting every foe.
    I fear no stormy weather,
    With You I have no woe.
    You'll offer me safekeeping
    Within Your tent of love,
    From danger I'm protected
    By sheltering wings above.

3.   My prayers You have heeded,
    Your grace bestowed on me.
    Who holds Your name in honor
    Receives Your legacy.
    So grant long life to those who
    Devote themselves to You,
    Year after year preserve them
    And send Your blessings too.

4.   Before the face of Heaven
    Let them forever be!
    For God's unending mercy
    Lasts to eternity.
    And so I'll sing a melody
    Just as I promised You,
    My praise a gift to You shall be
    Day after day anew.

Melody: French Psalter, Lyon 1547

Erna and Edith (ca. 1899 or 1900)

An outing in 1911 with friends and family. Edith is front row, left; Rosa front row, right; Edith's sister Erna is behind Edith; Auguste Stein, Edith's mother, is at top of picture right rear.

The following four short poems are designated by the author as "Sentenzen im Monat Juni 1940," ("Aphorisms in the month of June 1940"). These aphorisms may have been recited in the evening, before retiring, as last reflections to accompany the sisters into the night. Edith may have spoken these aphorisms at times. Some of them she may have composed for such occasions. In view of the fact that the date of composition followed the occupation of the Netherlands by Germany in May 1940, they appear very relevant to the conditions prevailing at that time. The English translation begins on page 73.

+

Senkungen im Monat Juni 1940

I.

Es tritt der Herr die Kelter
Und rot ist Sein Gewand.
Er fegt mit eisernem Besen
Gewaltig über das Land.
Er kündet in Sturmesbrausen
Sein letztes Kommen an.
Wir hören das mächtige Sausen,
Der Vater allein weiß das Wann.

=

In Deinem Herzen wohnt der
    ew'ge Frieden.
Du möchtest ihn in alle
    Herzen gießen,
Du möchtest strömend in sie
    überfließen,
Doch findest keinen Eingang
    Du hienieden.

Sie haben für Dein leises Pochen
    kein Ohren,
Drum mußt Du mit dem
    schweren Hammerschlagen.
Nach langer Nacht erst wird
    der Morgen tagen,
In harten Wehen wird Dein
    Reich geboren...

Wer wird uns Führer sein aus
    Nacht zum Lichte?
Wie wird der Schrecken enden?
Wo trifft die Sünder das Straf-
    gericht?
Wann wird sich das Schicksal
    wenden?

Der am Ölberg in blutigem Angst-
    schweiß rang
Mit dem Vater in heißem Flehen:
Er ist es, dem der Sieg gelang,
Da entschied sich das Welt-
    geschehen.

Dort fallet nieder und betet an
Und fragt nicht mehr:
    Wer? Wie? Wo? Wann?

IV.

Laßt uns nicht richten,
    daß wir nicht gerichtet werden!
Uns alle trügt der Dinge äuß'rer
                    Schein.
Wir sehen (Rätselbilder hier
                auf Erden.
Der Schöpfer einzig kennt
        das wahre Sein.

Als Jesus in Angst geriet, betete er noch inständiger.

Lk 22, 44

SENTENZEN IM MONAT JUNI, 1940.

I.

Es tritt der Herr die Kelter
Und rot ist sein Gewand.
Er fegt mit eisernem Besen
Gewaltig über das Land.
Er kündet in Sturmesbrausen
Sein letztes Kommen an.
Wir hören das mächtige Sausen,
Der Vater allein weiss das Wann.

II.

In Deinem Herzen wohnt der ew'ge Frieden.
Du möchtest ihn in alle Herzen giessen,
Du möchtest strömend in sie überfliessen,
Doch findest keinen Eingang Du hinieden.

Sie haben für Dein leises Pochen keine Ohren,
Drum musst Du mit dem schweren Hammer schlagen.
Nach langer Nacht erst wird der Morgen tagen,
In harten Wehen wird Dein Reich geboren.

III.

Wer wird uns Führer sein aus Nacht zum Licht?
Wer wird den Schrecken enden?
Wo trifft die Sünder das Strafgericht?
Wann wird sich das Schicksal wenden?

Der am Ölberg in blutigem Angstschweiss rang
Mit dem Vater in heissem Flehen:
Er ist es, dem der Sieg gelang;
Da entschied sich das Weltgeschehen.
Dort fallet nieder und betet an
Und fragt nicht mehr:
Wer? Wie? Wo? Wann?

In his anguish he (Jesus) prayed even more earnestly.

Luke 22:44.

APHORISMS IN THE MONTH OF JUNE 1940.

I.

The Lord is stomping grapes,
And blood-red is His gown.
He sweeps with broom of iron
Through hamlet and through town.
Proclaims in the storm's resounding
That He will come again,
We hear the awesome pounding.
Our Father alone knows when.

II.

Within Your heart lives peace eternal.
You want to pour it into our hearts.
And into each of them You want to flow,
But there is no opening where You can go.

When You knock gently, they give no ear.
A hammer's blows they will surely hear.
When the long night is past, morning will dawn,
In painful labor Your kingdom's born.

III.

From night to light who'll be our guide?
How will the horror end?
Where will the sinners be justly tried,
When will our fortunes mend?

From the Mount of Olives His anguished plea
To the Father in Heaven He hurled.
His agony gained Him the victory,
Determined the fate of the world.
There prostrate yourselves and pray, and then
Ask no more: Who? How? Where? or When?

IV.

Lasst uns nicht richten,
Dass wir nicht gerichtet werden!
Uns alle trügt der Dinge äuss'rer Schein.
Wir sehen Rätselbilder hier auf Erden,
Der Schöpfer einzig kennt das wahre Sein.

IV.

Judge not lest you be judged in turn,
Appearances cloud our view,
We guess at the truth, but only learn
God alone knows what is true.

Herr, rette uns! Wir gehen zugrunde!

Mt 8, 25.

AM STEUER.

1940

Herr, stürmisch sind die Wellen,
Und dunkel ist die Nacht,
Willst Du sie nicht erhellen
Für mich, die einsam wacht?

Halt fest die Hand am Steuer
Und sei getrost und still.
Dein Schifflein ist mir teuer,
Zum Ziel ich's lenken will.

Hab nur mit treuen Sinnen
Stets auf den Kompass acht,
Der hilft das Ziel gewinnen
Durch Stürme und durch Nacht.

Die Nadel zittert leise
Und steht dann wieder still,
Dass Richtung sie Dir weise,
Wohin die Fahrt ich will.

Sei drum getrost und stille;
Es führt durch Sturm und Nacht
Getreu Dich Gottes Wille,
Wenn das Gewissen wacht.

"Save us, Lord, we are going down!"

Matthew 8:25.

AT THE HELM.

1940.

Fierce are the waves, Lord, rough the seas,
And dark, so dark the night.
I beg of you to grant me, please,
On lonely vigil, light.

Then steer your ship with steady arm,
Trust me and rest your soul.
Your little boat I'll keep from harm,
I'll guide it toward its goal.

Be firm of purpose as you keep
The compass e'er in view.
Through stormy night you'll cross the deep,
'twill help you to steer true.

The needle trembles faintly, then
Holds steady and prevails,
It points your way and guides you when
I, God, direct your sails.

Be therefore steadfast, calm and true,
Your God is at your side.
Through storm and night He'll see you through
With conscience as your guide.

Mother Johanna of Beek, later Echt, added the year 1940 at the head of this poem and gave a copy of the handwritten text to Sr. Maria Amata Neyer OCD, Curator of the Edith-Stein-Archiv in the Carmel "Maria vom Frieden" in Cologne.

Gott ist uns Zuflucht und Kraft,
herrlich erwiesen als Helfer in der Bedrängnis.

Psalm 46

1. In al - ler Stür- me To - ben bist
Dich, star - ker Gott, wir lo - ben, der

du, Herr, un - sre Kraft. Si - cher
stets uns Hil - fe schafft.

ste - hen wir und ver - trau - en dir, wenn

auch die Er - de bebt, das Meer sich hoch er - hebt.

2. Wenn seine Wasser schwellen, der Berge Feste wankt,
wird Freude uns erhellen. Die Gottesstadt dir dankt. In
ihr weilest du, gibst ihr sichre Ruh. Es schützt ein starker
Strom den hehren Gottesdom.

3. Im Wahn die Völker toben, es stürzt der Stolzen Pracht,
da Gott die Stimm erhoben wie mit des Donners Macht.
Seht, mit uns ist Gott! Herr, Gott Sabaoth, du bist uns
Heil und Licht, drum fürchten wir uns nicht.

4. Kommt alle her, zu sehen die Wunder seiner Kraft!
Die Fehde muß vergehen, wo er den Frieden schafft. Speer
und Schild zerbricht unter seinem Licht. Der Herr Gott
Sabaoth hilft uns aus aller Not.

Weise: Adolf Lohmann

God is our shelter, our strength,
ever ready to help in time of trouble.

Psalm 46:1.

1. Whenever storms are roaring,
   You Lord, are our support.
   We praise You, God, imploring,
   You guide us safe to port.
   Safe, secure we stand,
   Trusting hold Your hand,
   Though the mountains quake
   Mighty oceans break.

2. When swelling waters frighten
   When solid mountains sway,
   Joy comes our life to lighten.
   Our thanks to You we say.
   In Your city dwell,
   Keep her safe and well.
   A mighty river shelters
   God's lofty citadel.

3. The nations rage in frenzy,
   The splendor of the proud
   Falls when God speaks with mighty voice
   No thunder is so loud.
   God is with us here.
   Lord of hosts, You're near,
   Our light and our salvation.
   Therefore we have no fear.

4. Come here, that you may see them,
   The wonders of His might
   Discord must surely vanish
   Where He brings peace and light.
   Spear and mighty shield
   To His light must yield
   The Lord God indeed
   Rescues all in need.

Melody: Adolf Lohmann

Mit seinen Flügeln beschirmt er dich, unter seinen
Fittichen bist du geborgen, seine Treue ist dir ein
schützender Schild.

Psalm 91

AN GOTT DEN VATER.

Segne der Leidbedrückten tiefgebeugten Sinn,
Der tiefen Seelen schwere Einsamkeit,
Das unruhvolle Sein der Menschen
Und Leid, das eine Seele keiner Schwesternseele je vertraut.

Und jenen Zug der nächt'gen Schwärmer segne,
Die unbekannter Wege Spuk nicht scheuen.
Die Not der Menschen segne, die zur Stunde sterben,
Gib ihnen, guter Gott, ein friedlich, selig End.

Segne die Herzen all; die trüben, Herr, vor allen.
Den Kranken Lind'rung gib; Gequälten, Frieden.
Die ihre Lieb' zu Grabe trugen, lehr vergessen,
Lass auf der ganzen Erd kein Herz in Sündenpein.

Seg'ne die Frohen, Herr, In Deiner Hut bewahr' sie.
Von mir nahmst Du noch nie der Trauer Kleid.
Es lastet manchmal schwer auf meinen müden Schultern—
Doch gibst Du Kraft, so trag ich's büssend bis ans Grab.

Dann segne meinen Schlaf, den Schlaf von allen Toten.
Gedenke, was Dein Sohn in Todesangst für mich litt.
Dein gross Bramherzigsein für alle Menschennöte
Gibt allen Toten Ruh in Deinem ew'gen Frieden.

He covers you with his feathers,
and you find shelter underneath his wings. . .
his faithfulness (is a) shield and buckler.

Psalm 91:4

TO GOD, THE FATHER.

Bless the mind deeply troubled
Of the sufferers,
The heavy loneliness of profound souls
The restlessness of human beings,
The sorrow which no soul ever confides
To a sister soul.

And bless the passage of moths at night,
Who do not shun spectres on paths unknown.
Bless the distress of men
Who die within the hour,
Grant them, loving God, a peaceful, blessed end.

Bless all the hearts, the clouded ones, Lord, above all,
Bring healing to the sick.
To those in torture, peace.
Teach those who had to carry their beloved to the grave, to
    forget.
Leave none in agony of guilt on all the earth.

Bless the joyous ones, O Lord, and keep them under Your
    wing. —
My mourning clothes you never yet removed.
At times my tired shoulders bear a heavy burden.
But give me strength, and I'll bear it
In penitence to the grave.

Then bless my sleep, the sleep of all the dead.
Remember what Your son suffered for me in agony of death.
Your great mercy for all human needs
Gives rest to all the dead in Your eternal peace.

It is assumed that this poem was written in 1939, possibly
for a memorial service for the dead. The penciled original is
written on very thin paper which had typescript on its verso.
The photostatic copy is hardly legible and shows signs of
many corrections and erasures. It seems to have been composed under the stresses of war, paper shortage and perhaps
in haste.

Much loving attention was obviously lavished on this charmingly illustrated little booklet, which most likely was a gift for the Prioress in Echt. It is dated Pentecost 1942. Its seven stanzas were intended for the Pentecost novenas, to be recited during the period of preparing for the Feast of Pentecost. As a last poetic message before Edith Stein's deportation and death as a victim of the Holocaust, it is most moving. It, too, was a gift to the Cologne Carmel from Sister Johanna, who died about 1972. Since 1978, the original is in the manuscript collection of the Vatican Library in Rome. Sister Amata relates that while the beatification process concerning Edith Stein was pending, the Vatican requested the Cologne Carmel to donate an original document by the hand of Edith Stein to the Vatican Library. The English translation begins on page 93.

✝

7
Strahlen
aus
einer
Ringst norene.

Pfingsten 1942

I.

Wer bist Du, süßes Licht, das mich erfüllt
Und meines Herzens Dunkelheit erleuchtet?
Du leitest mich gleich einer Mutter Hand,
Und ließest Du mich los, so wüßte keinen
                    Schritt ich mehr zu geh'n.
Du bist der Raum, der rund mein Sein um-
                    schließt und in sich birgt,
Aus Dir entlassen entsänk' es in den Abgrund
        des Nichts, aus dem Du es zum Licht erhöbst.
Du, näher mir als ich mir selbst
Und innerlicher als mein Innerstes —
Und doch ungreifbar und unfaßbar
Und jeden Namen sprengend:
        Heiliger Geist —
                    Ewige Liebe.

I.

Bist Du das süße Manna nicht, das aus des Sohnes
Herzen

In mein Herz überströmt,

Der Engel und der Sel'gen Speise?

Er, der vom Tod zu neuem Leben sich erhob,

Er hat auch mich zu neuem Leben auferweckt
vom Schlaf des Todes,

Und neues Leben gibt Er mir von Tag zu Tag,

Und einst soll seine Fülle mich durchfluten,

Leben von Deinem Leben— ja Du selbst:

Heiliger Geist —

Ewiges Leben.

VII.

Bist Du der Strahl, der von des ew'gen Richters
       Thron hernieder zuckt
Und einbricht in die Nacht der Seele,
Die nie sich selbst erkannt?
Barmherzig-unerbittlich dringt er in ver-
       borg'ne Falten.
Erschreckt vom Anblick ihrer selbst
Gewährt sie Raum heiliger Furcht,
  Dem Anfang jener Weisheit,
Die aus der Höhe kommt und in der Höhe
       uns fest ver ankert:
Deinem Wirken das neu uns schafft –
  Heiliger Geist –

    all durch dringender Strahl!

IV.

Bist Du des Geistes Fülle und der Kraft,
Womit das Lamm die Siegel löst
Von Gottes ew'gem Ratschluß?
Von Dir getrieben reiten des Gerichtes
          Boten durch die Welt
Und scheiden mit scharfem Schwert
Das Reich des Lichtes von dem Reich der
            Nacht.
Dann wird der Himmel neu und neu die
            Erde
Und alles kommt an seinen rechten Ort
Durch Deinen Hauch:

     Heiliger Geist-

        Siegende Kraft.

87

V.

Bist Du der Meister, der den ew'gen Dom erbaut,
Der von der Erde durch die Himmel ragt?
Von Dir belebt erheben sich die Säulen hoch
      empor
Und stehen unverrückbar fest.
Bezeichnet mit dem ew'gen Namen Gottes
Recken sie sich hinauf ins Licht
Und tragen die gewalt'ge Kuppel,
Die den heil'gen Dom bekrönend abschließt,
Dein weltumfassendes Werk,

　　Heiliger Geist –

　　　　Gottes bildende Hand.

VII.

Bist Du es, der den klaren Spiegel schuf
Zu nächst des Allerhöchsten Thron,
Gleich einem Meere von Kristall,
Darin die Gottheit liebend sich beschaut?
Du neigst Dich über Deiner Schöpfung schön-
stes Werk,
Und strahlend leuchtet Dir Dein eig'ner Glanz
entgegen
Und aller Wesen reine Schönheit
Vereinigt in der lieblichen Gestalt
Der Jungfrau, Deiner makellosen Braut:

    Heiliger Geist –

        Schöpfer des All.

IX.

Bist Du das süße Lied der Liebe und der
                    heil'gen Scheu,
Das ewig tönt um des Dreifalt'gen Thron,
Das aller Wesen reinen Klang in sich ver-
                              mählt?
Der Einklang, der zum Haupt die Glieder
                              fügt,
Darin ein jedes seines Seins geheimen
                                    Sinn
                    beseligt findet
Und jubelnd ausströmt,
Frei gelöst in Deinem Strömen:
        Heiliger Geist –
                    Ewiger Jubel.

Alleluja

Der Geist und die Braut sprechen: "Komm!" Und
wer es hört, soll sprechen: "Komm!" Und wen es
dürstet, der komme, wer will, der empfange lebendiges Wasser umsonst.

Offb 22, 17

SIEBEN STRAHLEN AUS EINER PFINGSTNOVENE.

I.

Wer bist Du, süsses Licht, das mich erfüllt
Und meines Herzens Dunkelheit erleuchtet?
Du leitest mich gleich einer Mutter Hand,
Und liessest Du mich los,
So wüsste keinen Schritt ich mehr zu gehn.
Du bist der Raum,
Der rund mein Sein umschliesst und in sich birgt,
Aus Dir entlassen sänk' es in den Abgrund
Des Nichts, aus dem Du es zum Sein erhobst.
Du, näher mir als ich mir selbst
Und innerlicher als mein Innerstes —
Und doch ungreifbar und unfassbar
Und jeden Name sprengend:

Heiliger Geist —
Ewige Liebe!

The Spirit and the Bride say, "Come."
Let everyone who listens answer, "Come."
Then let all who are thirsty come;
all who want it may have the water of life
and have it free.

Revelation 22:17

SEVEN BEAMS FROM A PENTECOST NOVENA.

Pentecost, 1942.

I.

Who are You, sweet light that fills me
And illumines the darkness of my heart?
You guide me like a mother's hand,
And if You let me go, I could not take
Another step.
You are the space
That surrounds and contains my being.
Without You it would sink into the abyss
Of nothingness from which You raised it into being.
You, closer to me than I to myself,
More inward than my innermost being—
And yet unreachable, untouchable,
And bursting the confines of any name:

Holy spirit—
Eternal love!

II.

Bist Du das süsse Manna nicht,
Das aus des Sohnes Herzen
In mein Herz überströmt,
Der Engel und der Sel'gen Speise?
Er, der vom Tod zum Leben sich erhob,
Er hat auch mich zu neuem Leben auferweckt
Vom Schlaf des Todes.
Und neues Leben gibt er mir von Tag zu Tag.
Und einst soll seine Fülle mich durchfluten,
Leben von Deinem Leben—ja, Du selbst:

      Heiliger Geist—
             Ewiges Leben!

III.

Bist Du der Strahl,
Der von des ew'gen Richters Thron herniederzuckt
Und einbricht in die Nacht der Seele,
Die nie sich selbst erkannt?
Barmherzig—unerbittlich dringt er in verborg'ne Falten.
Erschreckt vom Anblick ihrer selbst
Gewährt sie Raum heiliger Furcht.
Dem Anfang jener Weisheit,
Die aus der Höhe kommt und in der Höhe uns fest verankert:
Deinem Wirken, das neu uns schafft,

      Heiliger Geist—
             Alldurchdringender Strahl!

II.

Are You not the sweet manna
Which flows from the heart of the Son
Into mine,
Food for angels and for the blessed?
He who from death to life arose,
Has awakened me, too, to new life,
From the sleep of death,
New life he gives me day by day.
Some day his abundance will completely flow through me,
Life of Your life—yes, You Yourself:

Holy spirit—
                    Eternal life!

III.

Are You the ray
That flashes from the Eternal Judge's throne
To pierce into the night of my soul,
Which never knew itself?
Merciful, yet unrelenting, it penetrates the hidden crevices.
The soul takes fright at sight of her own self,
Makes room for holy awe,
For the beginning of that wisdom
Descending from on high,
And anchoring us securely in the heights,—
For Your workings, which create us anew:

Holy Spirit—
                    All-penetrating ray!

IV.

Bist Du des Geistes Fülle und der Kraft,
Womit das Lamm die Siegel löst
Von Gottes ew'gem Ratschluss.
Von Dir getrieben reiten des Gerichtes Boten durch die Welt
Und scheiden mit scharfem Schwert
Das Reich des Lichtes vom dem Reich der Nacht.
Dann wird der Himmel neu und neu die Erde,
Und alles kommt an seinen rechten Ort
Durch Deinen Hauch:

Heiliger Geist
Siegende Kraft!

V.

Bist Du der Meister, der den ew'gen Dom erbaut,
Der von der Erde durch den Himmel ragt?
Von Dir belebt erheben sich die Säulen hoch empor
Und stehen unverrückbar fest.
Bezeichnet mit dem Ew'gen Namen Gottes
Recken sie sich auf ins Licht,
Die Kuppel tragend, die den heil'gen Dom bekrönend abschliesst,
Dein weltumspannendes Werk,

Heiliger Geist—
Gottes bildende Hand.

VI.

Bist Du es, der den klaren Spiegel schuf,
Zunächst des Allerhöchsten Thron,
Gleich einem Meere von Kristall,
Darin die Gottheit liebend sich beschaut?
Du neigst Dich über Deiner Schöpfung schönstes Werk,
Und strahlend leuchtet Dir Dein eigner Glanz entgegen
Und aller Wesen reine Schönheit,
Vereinigt in der lieblichen Gestalt
Der Jungfrau, Deiner makellosen Braut:

Heiliger Geist—
Schöpfer des All.

IV.

Are You the wealth of spirit and of power
By which the Lamb loosens the seals
From God's eternal decree?
Driven by You the messengers of judgment
Ride through the world
And with sharp sword divide
The reign of light from the reign of night.
Then the Heavens are renewed, and new the earth,
And through Your breath
Everything finds its rightful place:

> Holy Spirit—
>
> > Conquering power!

V.

Are You the master who builds the eternal dome
Rising from earth and through to very Heaven?
The columns, enlivened by You, rise high
And stand firm, immovable.
Marked with the eternal name of God,
They reach high up into the light,
Bearing the cupola, which crowns the holy dome,
Your work encompassing the universe,

> Holy Spirit—
>
> > God's shaping hand.

VI.

Are You the one who made the mirror bright,
Which stands beside the throne of the Almighty
Just like a sea of crystal
Wherein the Godhead views Himself with love?
You bend o'er the most marvelous of Your creations
And beaming shines Your splendor back to you.
The pure beauty of all beings
United in the lovely form of
The virgin, Your flawless bride:

> Holy Spirit—
>
> > Creator of the World.

VII.

Bist Du das süsse Lied der Liebe und der heiligen Scheu,
Das ewig tönt um des Dreifalt'gen Thron,
Das aller Wesen reinen Klang in sich vermählt?
Der Einklang, der zum Haupt die Glieder fügt,
Darin ein jeder seines Seins geheimen Sinn beseligt findet
Und jubelnd ausströmt
Frei gelöst in Deinem Strömen:

Heiliger Geist—
Ewiger Jubel!

VII.

Are You the sweet song of love, and of holy awe,
Resounding ever round God's throne triune,
Which unifies the pure tone of all beings,
Within itself?
The harmony which fits the limbs to the head,
So that each blissfully finds the secret meaning
Of His being,
And exudes it with gladness freely dissolved
In Your streams:

       Holy Spirit—

              Eternal jubilation.

Singt unserm Gott, ja singt! Singt unserm König,
ja singt! Denn König der ganzen Erde ist Gott!
Stimmt an ein festliches Lied!

Psalm 47

1. Jauchzt, ihr Völ-ker, fröh-lich seid!

Ju-belt dem Herrn, al-le Lan-de weit!

Groß und er-ha-ben und furcht-bar an Macht

ü-ber den Erd-kreis als Kö-nig er wacht.

Rings-um be-zwang er die Völ-ker all.

Jauchzt ihm zum Dan-ke mit Ju-bel-schall!

2. Uns verlieh sein Erbe er, Freude an Israel hat der Herr.
   Gott ist gestiegen zur Höhe empor, jubelnd begrüßt von
   Posaunen im Chor. Preist unsern Gott, unserm König
   singt! Durch alle Lande sein Loblied klingt.

3. Gott ist Herrscher aller Welt. Über die Erde hoch ragt
   sein Zelt. Fürsten der Völker, sie strömen herbei zu unserm
   Gott, daß der ihre er sei. Mit ihm erheben sie sich empor.
   Sonne gleich strahlet ihr mächtger Chor.

Weise: Adolf Lohmann

Clap your hands, all you peoples,
acclaim God with shouts of joy. . .
God is king of the whole world;
play your best in his honor!

Psalm 47:1-2

1. Rejoice, ye nations, shout with mirth!
   Rejoice in the Lord all the earth!
   Great and lofty and awesome in power
   Above the globe our king does tower.
   Subdued the nations all around,
   So greet Him with thankful, joyful sound.

2. To us He gave His legacy,
   Delight in Israel has he.
   God mounted His throne high in the air.
   A chorus of trumpets greets Him there.
   Praise our God, chant an ode to our King,
   All through the lands let praises ring.

3. God rules over all the world,
   High o'er the earth His tent's unfurled.
   Princes of nations, they stream to His throne,
   Acclaiming our God their very own.
   With Him to the lofty heavens they rise
   Their chorus shines like the sun in the skies.

Melody: Adolf Lohmann

This is the last extant photo of Edith Stein.

A Martyr of Auschwitz

A Martyr of Auschwitz

On May 1, 1987, Sister Teresa Benedicta of the Cross was beatified for a holy life that ended in martyrdom at Auschwitz. The ceremony was held at the Sports Stadium in Cologne, West Germany, and my husband and I, Jews and proud of our Judaism, were among the invited guests, along with some 20 of our relatives. Teresa Benedicta was Edith Stein, my mother's youngest sister.

Aunt Edith, or Tante Edith as I have always called her, was only 19 months younger than my mother, Erna, and they were always close. They shared a bedroom growing up in Germany at the turn of the century and attended the same schools through their first year of college. When my aunt converted to Roman Catholicism, she first confided in Erna, begging her to break the news to their widowed mother.

And now my aunt, who on January 26, 1987, was declared venerable, has taken the second of three steps toward possible sainthood, a long and by no means inevitable process. Joseph Cardinal Höffner of Cologne wrote to say that he "would be happy to be able to greet" my husband, Alfred, and me at the ceremony, which marked the first beatification of a Jewish convert in modern times.

As we prepared for the event, we did so amid the backdrop of a controversy precipitated by an often-asked question, raised among others by James Raphael Baaden, a London-based Jewish writer working on a biography of Edith Stein. In a letter to the Sacred Congregation for the Causes of Saints, which considers the candidates proposed for sainthood, Baaden asked whether Edith Stein died as she did because she was a Jew or because she was a Catholic. If the former, as he contends on the basis of Nazi policy to kill all Jews irrespective of their conversion to other religions, how could she be beatified as a Christian martyr? In his reply, the Rev. Ambrogio Eszer, postulator of Edith Stein's beatification cause, said, "To me it is very clear that the motive of the Nazi action was *odium fidei,* hatred against the church (sic)," which is required to prove the genuineness of a martyrdom.

I went to Cologne, but I went with mixed feelings. My memories of the past inevitably intruded upon the present. My brother, Ernst, did not wish to lend his presence, and thus his implicit approval, to a proceeding the motives of which he questioned.

Edith Stein, the last of the 11 children of my grandparents Siegfried and Auguste Stein, was born in Breslau, Germany (now Wroclaw, Poland), on Oct. 12, 1891. It was Yom Kippur, the holiest day of the Jewish year. Grandmother, a pious woman, was overjoyed by the coincidence. A year and a half later, Edith's father died, leaving her mother to rear the children and manage the family lumber business.

Edith was a bright child, and excelled in her studies. When she was 19, she entered the University of Breslau. From Breslau she went on to Göttingen University to study with Edmund Husserl, the father of phenomenology. When World War I broke out in 1914, my aunt joined the Red Cross and became a nurse's aide. Six months later, she resumed her studies, this time at the University of Freiburg, where Husserl had gone. There she obtained her doctorate, with highest honors, and became Husserl's assistant.

Throughout her student years, Edith was spiritually adrift. Though my grandmother was a devout Jew, her children had little knowledge of Jewish matters. The boys knew some Hebrew, enough to become Bar Mitzvah, but the girls had almost no Jewish education. Thus, when Edith Stein tells us in her autobiography, "Life in a Jewish Family" (first published in Belgium in 1965; American edition, 1986), that she lost her faith at the age of 15, we must keep in mind that it was not out of a thorough familiarity with Judaism. It is intriguing, however futile, to speculate what might have happened to her spiritual development had she turned to a more intensive study of Judaism instead of Catholicism.

Tante Edith was surrounded by many professors and fellow students who had left Judaism and embraced Christianity, some for career advancement in a time of limited opportunities for Jews, others, such as herself, for purely spiritual reasons. Published accounts state that her reading of the life of St. Teresa of Avila impelled my aunt to convert to Catholicism, but there has always been speculation among her biographers and within the family about what else may have affected her decision. A personal crisis? A romantic disappointment? In any event, she was baptized a Catholic on New Year's Day, 1922.

A 1911 photograph. Edith is in foreground with friends and (top right) Edith's sister Erna, the mother of Susanne Batzdorff.

The new convert yearned for a cloistered life, but her priestly mentors advised against it, to spare her aging mother additional grief. My aunt yielded, and accepted a teaching position at the lyceum and teacher's college of St. Magdalena, in Speyer. She also wrote and lectured widely on education and the role of the Catholic woman. Although not a militant feminist, she strongly favored more options for women, both in religious and secular life.

In 1928 she translated the letters of John Henry Cardinal Newman from English to German. The following year, she published a comparison of the philosophy of Thomas Aquinas and the phenomenology of Edmund Husserl. Her most ambitious work begun in that period was "Finite and Eternal Being," but it was not finished until 1936.

She was appointed a lecturer in 1932 at the faculty of the German Institute for Scientific Pedagogy, in Münster, an institution under Catholic auspices. Within a year, however, Hitler came to power, and my aunt was dismissed because of her Jewish background. The time was ripe for her to fulfill a long-cherished dream, to join the Discalced Carmelites, a cloistered order whose name derives from their wearing only sandals, never shoes.

For her, it was the right moment to take this step. Not, however, for her Jewish family. She could not have picked a worse time to distance herself from us as Jews, the newly designated pariahs of German society. Hitler's plan of ridding Germany of Jews was already being implemented. Christianity, which Edith had chosen to embrace, was in our eyes in 1933 the religion of our persecutors. For Grandmother Stein, it was the severest blow imaginable. Her daughter Edith was about to enter a cloister in Cologne, a contemplative order with strict rules. She would not be allowed to come home for a visit, ever, and though she could receive visitors, her 84-year-old mother, who had given up all traveling, would never see her again.

Tante Edith had always occupied a special place in the family. She was, for the most part, an absentee aunt, even before she became a Carmelite, but she wrote regularly to all her nieces and nephews. And my brother and I enjoyed reading the humorous playlet she composed for our parents' wedding, and participating with our cousins in the dance skit she prepared for Grandmother Stein's 80th birthday.

When she came to visit, her presence immediately made itself felt. As my brother once put it, she brought a holiday atmosphere with her. To us, she was not a figure of other-worldly scholarly solemnity, but a friend with a delightful sense of humor who could be relied on for annual visits. Until she became a Carmelite nun, that is.

Dominican monastery of St. Magdalena, Speyer, where Edith Stein taught.

In the summer of 1933, not long before she entered the cloister, Aunt Edith began writing "Life in a Jewish Family," which she hoped would show German readers that Jews were people like themselves, that they were rooted in the German past and loyal to their country. It was futile, for Nazi ideology was not amenable to reason. But I am glad she recorded this family history, for it is an authentic statement about her life.

From her collection of books, which remained in Grandmother's house, I received a volume on each birthday as a gift from my aunt. I still cherish these mementos, which include Rainer Maria Rilke's "Stories of God" and a collection of Hans Christian Andersen. Another treasured keepsake is a message she sent me on Aug. 20, 1933, just before she became a nun. It is a quotation from the 27th Psalm. In a time of fear and uncertainty, a time for me of confusion and doubt, she had written:

"The Lord is my light and my salvation; whom shall I fear?"

I last saw my aunt that October. I was then 12 years old. My younger brother and I had only recently been told about her conversion to Catholicism. We may have been children, but we were very much aware of developments in Germany as they affected Jews. By becoming a Catholic, our aunt had abandoned her people. By entering a cloister, she was proclaiming to the outside world her desire to dissociate herself from the Jewish people. That is how we saw it, and that is how I expressed it to her that October afternoon when she and I chanced to meet at the dentist's.

It was a rare opportunity for me to speak to her alone. I felt awkward and embarrassed, for it was not considered seemly then for children to address grown-ups in a challenging manner. I probably was not very articulate, and my persuasive powers could not have been impressive. But it was characteristic of my aunt that she did not take my words lightly, nor did she condescend.

She remained gravely attentive throughout and then replied that she did not see the step she was about to take as a betrayal. Entering a convent could not, she said, guarantee her safety, nor could it shut out the reality of the world outside. As a Carmelite, she said, she would remain a part of her family and of the Jewish people. To her, that was entirely logical; to us, her Jewish relatives, it could never be a convincing argument. Despite our love for her, a gap had opened between us that would never be bridged.

Her letters from the Cologne Carmel, though written in the familiar hand, were now signed "Benedicta," signaling a deliberate distancing from her past, from an identity rooted in Judaism, from the name given to her by her Jewish parents.

That my aunt did not feel she had abandoned her fellow Jews was evident in the written appeal she sent before entering the cloister to Pope Pius XI, asking for an encyclical condemning the anti-Semitic policies of the National Socialist Government in Germany. Because of her ties to both Catholicism and Judaism and her respected position in Catholic academic circles, she hoped to intercede and effect a dramatic change through moral suasion.

Her bold act proved that she was, indeed, still loyal to her Jewish family and heritage. In a letter written in October 1938 to the Mother Superior of an Ursuline convent in Dorsten, she says:

"I cannot help thinking again and again of Queen Esther, who was taken from her people for the express purpose of standing before the King for her people. I am a very poor and helpless little Esther, but the King who chose me is infinitely great and merciful."

Her failure to enlist the sympathy of the Holy Father must have been a grievous disappointment.

Right after Kristallnacht, Nov. 9, 1938, when the Nazi persecution of the Jews assumed increasing virulence with the smashing of the windows of Jewish properties, the burning of synagogues and wholesale arrests, my aunt and her superiors decided it would be safer for her and their Carmelite community if she were transferred abroad. On New Year's Eve, she was taken to the Netherlands, and received by the Carmel in Echt. There she continued writing her autobiographical volume and began work on a book about the life and work of St. John of the Cross. It remained unfinished, because the Gestapo took her away on Aug. 2, 1942, together with her older sister Rosa. Inspired by Edith's example, Rosa had converted to Catholicism following their mother's death in 1936, and had been living as a lay person in the extern quarters of the cloister since 1939. Their arrest during a roundup of Catholics of Jewish origin was in retaliation for a forceful protest by the Dutch bishops against the anti-Semitic outrages of the Nazi occupation forces.

I do not believe that Edith Stein sought martyrdom. On the one hand, there are her assertions offering up her life for the church, for world peace, even for the unbelief of the Jewish people. On the other hand, her actions give proof of her determination to save her life and that of her sister Rosa.

When the Carmel at Le Pâquier, in the Swiss canton of Fribourg, offered her asylum but said it could not take her sister Rosa, Tante Edith declined. This was the only instance in which she refused outright to be rescued.

From Westerbork, the Dutch staging post for the concentration camps, my aunt still urged, in a hastily scribbled message to her

The synagogue (called "the New Synagogue") where the Stein family worshipped and where Edith and her mother went on the occasion she mentions in her essay. The synagogue was burned and the remains dynamited on November 9-10, 1938 (Kristallnacht) by the Nazis. There is now a parking lot on the site.

Mother Superior in Echt, that efforts on behalf of herself and Rosa be continued. And finally, the heart-rending notes she dropped from freight-train compartments as she passed through towns where she had once lived and might still be remembered, testify to her last frantic attempts to avert her doom—or at least to help future chroniclers of these dismal events to track her final journey. She and her sister Rosa were gassed to death in Auschwitz, probably on Aug. 9, 1942. Of those Roman Catholics who died in the death camps, one, the Rev. Maksymilian Kolbe, a Polish priest who volunteered in Auschwitz to die in another man's stead, has been elevated to sainthood.

As I study her writings, her letters, her poems I sometimes feel that I come closer to understanding her than I could as a girl of twelve, when I had my last conversation with her. But what she really was, the essence of her life and death, will forever remain her secret.

After the war in Europe ended and my family, which had immigrated to the United States in 1939, learned the extent of the ravages that the Holocaust had wrought among our relatives, my mother grieved deeply for Edith, Rosa, a third sister, Frieda, and a brother, Paul, all victims of the Nazi death machine.

Tante Edith had, perhaps, been the closest to my mother's heart, because they were closest in age and were not only sisters, but also good friends. But in my mother's eyes, Edith did not wear a halo. I well recall my mother saying, "I would have preferred a thousand times a living sister to a dead saint."

I feel, as did my mother, who died in 1978, that Edith Stein was a human being who accomplished much, contributed to philosophical and religious literature, won the love and admiration of many and died a horrible death. Though she was a Catholic who embraced her chosen faith with joy and devotion, she was not, in the end, separated from those who had remained Jews and were killed because they were Jews.

This article first appeared, in slightly different form, in the *New York Times Magazine,* April 12, 1987, just prior to the Beatification of Edith Stein, Sister Teresia Benedicta a Cruce.

Edith and her sister Erna, with their nephew Gerhard Stein, son of their eldest brother, Paul (ca. 1905)

Catholics and Jews: Can We Bridge the Abyss?

It was a great honor to receive the 1988 Edith Stein Guild Award and especially to share it with my good friend Josephine Koeppel, O.C.D. Our work in connection with the translation of Edith Stein's autobiography [*Life in a Jewish Family* (ICS Publications, 1986)] first brought us together more than 10 years ago, and since then we have grown in mutual respect and understanding. I worked closely with her on editing and refining this translation and served as a resource for family and cultural milieu and authenticity.

That cooperation symbolizes, in a way, our endeavor to promote cooperation, mutual respect and understanding for human beings who may have different beliefs and ideologies, but who must live together in a troubled world.

In reflecting about the reasons for having been given the award, I recognize its connection with my particular effort concerning the life and work of my aunt Edith. While my mother was still living, she kept in touch with many people who were interested in Edith Stein, who wanted information of some kind or who were linked to Edith in some way. At times my mother received these people in her home; at times she wrote to them. She also tried to correct errors and misunderstandings found in publications about her sister. She was our family's link to the public. I have since taken over that role as best I can, maintaining a file of published material, letters, pictures and the like. I try to correct false impressions and factual errors. Obviously, I did not know my aunt as well as her own sister did, but there are many things I remember. I also lived in my grandmother's house for the first 12 years of my life and can thus testify to what family life in that house was like. Moreover, through my correspondence and published articles I try to interpret the Jewish viewpoint in the Catholic-Jewish dialogue.

I have learned two things of some importance:

1. The tremendous proliferation of "legendary material" and the liberties taken with historical fact are mindboggling. Stories that are

either wholly or partially untrue have been stated as fact and then repeated. To correct such a factual error is almost impossible, for it attains a stubborn life of its own and drives out the true fact.

This recognition leads me to say that if this is happening while eyewitnesses who remember the facts and can vouch for their accuracy are still alive, how much more fanciful will the legend grow in another few decades, after these eyewitnesses are gone? I counteract this tendency by providing corrective information, but it seems at times futile—like putting one's finger in the dike to stem the mighty tide. Even if errata are subsequently corrected, these corrections are not always seen by those who read the original story.

2. The job of achieving understanding between Christians and Jews must be ongoing. Constant effort, good will and diplomacy must be employed to further this goal. Those who agree that peaceful coexistence is desirable must work for it, but we must do so with our eyes open. It will not help to declare that differences between the faiths are unimportant, that there is really only one "Judeo-Christian ideology." If we do not comprehend where we differ, we will not discover what unites us. Wishful thinking is not a firm foundation to build on. Recognition of the facts of history and what they teach us is important. The cross, for instance, has a wholly different meaning for the Christian than for the Jew.

The Rev. Edward Flannery, in the introduction to his book *The Anguish of the Jews* (1965), tells of a young Jewish woman's reaction to seeing a huge illuminated cross at Christmas time: "That cross makes me shudder. It is like an evil presence."

In talking to her, Father Flannery learned why she saw fear and evil in a symbol that to him meant universal love and redemption. Her view was colored by centuries of suffering by Jews at the hands of Christians. Pogroms, inquisitions, forced conversions and crusades were perpetrated in the name of Christian zeal and caused death and destruction to thousands. And the most virulent tide of anti-Jewish action, under National Socialism, was able to build on a pre-existing foundation of Christian anti-Semitism that, regrettably, often emanated from the pulpit.

Even in our own time, here in the United States, we have such an example of the subversion of the cross as a symbol when the Ku Klux Klan uses that symbol of universal love to express bigotry and hatred.

As I told the press before and after my aunt's beatification, Edith's choice to become a Catholic was a blow because of what Christianity had done to the Jews in the past. Her entry into Carmel came at a moment when the Jews were threatened by Christians as never before.

116

The irony and tragedy of Edith Stein's life was that in following her conscience on the road to Christianity she felt that she was pursuing her Jewish path to its ultimate goal. But it is impossible, from the Jewish perspective, to see it that way. For Jews, the Christian faith is not the natural culmination of Judaism, but another path, another truth. We cannot accept the thesis that "the Old Covenant is fulfilled in the New." Judaism is a religious entity, a system of beliefs and teachings that carries its own fulfillment, its own messianic hope and goals. And thus a Jew who turns to Catholicism, in our view, is no longer a Jew. By his or her choice, that person has embarked on a spiritual journey that is no less valid to him but that cannot be seen by us as a further or higher continuation on the same path. Edith Stein tells us that by becoming a Catholic she felt truly Jewish for the first time in her life, but to her Jewish family it appeared that she had left the fold.

The irony does not end there. Even as she felt closer to her Jewish heritage, she was made to feel an outsider by her fellow Jews. She was also a target of the racial anti-Semitism of the Hitler regime. By its laws she was subject to the restrictions against Jews, whether they were Jews by accident of birth or by acknowledged allegiance. By the accident of Jewish ancestry, a person was subject to persecution and execution, regardless of whether he or she personally embraced the Jewish faith. Edith shared the fate of her Jewish "brothers and sisters," both literally and figuratively, in the gas chambers of Auschwitz. In death she was united with them, even though in life she had embarked on a different road.

We are poignantly aware of these contradictions, and they have contributed to the difficulties that arose out of the designation of Edith Stein as a Christian martyr. In correspondence with Victor Donovan, C.P., a long-time friend devoted to achieving greater closeness between Catholics and Jews, I stated: "In my family the truth jumps out at me dramatically, because Edith was not the only one of her family who was murdered in the Holocaust. With her was her sister Rosa (like Edith a convert to Catholicism, like her, arrested in the Carmelite monastery of Echt, Holland, deported and killed in Auschwitz on the same day as her sister, but rarely mentioned by the church) and besides these two, her brother Paul and his wife, her sister Frieda, and her niece Eva were likewise slaughtered."

Edith did not choose martyrdom. It was thrust upon her as it was thrust upon millions of Jews by the simple accident of their having been born Jewish.

The Jewish and the Christian view of martyrdom differ sharply. "I have set before you life and death, blessing and curse; therefore choose life...loving the Lord your God, obeying his voice and cleaving to him; for that means life to you and length of days" (Deut. 30, 19-20). And again: "You shall...keep my statutes and my ordinances, by doing which a man shall live" (Lev. 18:5).

In the words of Rabbi Daniel Landes, "After 2,000 years of Jewish suffering, martyrdom barely has a place in Jewish liturgy and is not extolled as the ideal."

In the Christian view, martyrdom has a different role. Each view is valid for its believer, but by claiming that they are identical, we force one into the Procrustean bed of the other, into a bed where it does not fit or can only be accommodated with great pain, twisting and distortion.

Understanding can never be achieved by glossing over or by one side trying to convince the other that it alone is in possession of the truth. Too much pain and suffering have occurred over the centuries because people have followed the motto: *Und willst Du nicht mein Bruder sein, So schlag ich Dir den Schädel ein.* ("If you refuse to be my brother, I smash your brains in.")

How much better to listen to our brothers' cry, to strive for the empathy that my aunt wrote about in her doctoral dissertation, to search for ways to help each other, to see the common humanity and grant to others the right to follow the path of their choice by which they reach our common goals.

Some time ago we commemorated the 50th anniversary of *Kristallnacht,* the Night of Broken Glass, Nov. 9-10, 1938. It was the opening of the violent phase of the Holocaust, the pogrom in which synagogues were destroyed and people were arrested and shipped to concentration camps by the thousands. We commemorate, we mourn, but we must stand together and vow to be more sensitive in the future to the cry of human beings, to refuse to join the howling mob, to heal and rescue rather than cast stones and firebrands, and to fight injustice wherever we may find it. That is a goal worth fighting for; that is a purpose to which we can all dedicate ourselves, regardless of race, color or religion.

So far, the church has not found any bona fide miracles attributable to Edith Stein. But if I may paraphrase Father Donovan, if the memory of Edith Stein can inspire us to such courage and such resolve, that may perhaps be miracle enough.

This article first appeared in *America,* March 11, 1989.

Edith Stein about 1913-14, as a philosophy student at Gottingen.

TANTE EDITH.

by Susanne M. Batzdorff.

A firm handshake,
A cloud-soft voice,
A gentle smile,
But cool, aloof.

Your nephews bow,
The nieces curtsy,
A bit in awe
Minding their manners.

This special aunt
Makes appearances
Only rarely, no more
Than twice a year.

Tante Edith has dimples
In her chin.
Her soft brown hair
Is combed straight back,
A bit too severely.
Are you afraid
To let any wisps
Or curls escape
From the straight and narrow?

In that long-ago time
You kept us at arm's length.
Your time was precious.
You were always writing
Or seeing visitors.
We remained outside
The heavy doors, which
Kept your voices muffled,
Strictly confidential.

Oh, Tante Edith,
We hardly knew you.
Who are you, really?
A mix of theology
and phenomenology?
Of Jewish ancestors
And priestly mentors?

A follower after
Strange gods?
What led you to worship
The Jew on the cross?

Grandmother's favorite,
My mother's playmate.
How do you fit
Into my family?
Where do you belong?

You puzzled your brothers
And sisters,
When you took the veil
Of Carmel.

Grandmother shook her head
And shed silent tears.
Her whole body shook
With soundless weeping
The day you left
To become a nun.

Four decades ago
They killed you in Auschwitz.
You left behind
Books about saints
About philosophers,
Lecture notes, letters.
But no explanations
Of the why and how
Of your life.

The Church is about
To beatify you.
What does that mean
To your Jewish family?

Grandmother could never
Have fathomed such things.
Perhaps she would flee
To the worn, yellowed pages
Of her prayerbook,
To find a psalm
For balance, for comfort.
But now she won't need to.
She's gone, you're gone.
No one is left
To help us, the living
Puzzle it out.

July, 1986.

Edith Stein's family. Back row, left to right: Arno (1879-1948), Else (1876-1956), Siegfried (1843-1893), Elfriede (1881-1942), Paul (1872-1943): front row, left to right: Rosa (1883-1942), Auguste (nee Courant, 1849-1936), Edith (1891-1936), Erna (1890-1978). Of the seven children, four fell victim to the Nazi holocaust — Paul, Elfriede, Rosa and Edith.

After the beatification ceremony. From left to right: Alfred Batzdorff, Susanne Batzdorff, Bernhard Rosenmoller (whose family were close friends of Edith Stein), Pope John Paul II, Cardinal Hoffner and Mr. Solzbacher, an aide to the cardinal.